ALPINE SKI MOUNTAINEERING

VOLUME 1: WESTERN ALPS

ABOUT THE AUTHOR

Bill O'Connor, author of this guidebook, is an internationally qualified (IFMGA) mountain and ski guide based in the Lake District. He spends up to eight months of the year abroad – at least three of which are spent off-piste skiing and touring in the Alps. A former Head of Outdoor Education at both Marlborough College and Loughborough University he has spent the last twenty-five years guiding in Britain, Europe and the Greater Ranges.

Bill is a member of the Alpine Club, Alpine Climbing Group and Alpine Ski Club, and is a Fellow of the Royal Geographical Society. When not 'out there doing it' he lectures, contributes articles and photographs to most of the leading outdoor publications in the UK and abroad, and runs his photographic library. He has contributed to numerous publications on mountaineering and has written several acclaimed books including an alpine guidebook to Mont Blanc, a book of scrambles in the Lake District and two volumes on Nepal including *The Trekking Peaks Of Nepal*.

He lives in Cumbria with Sallie, his wife, and two sons, William and Cameron, who are also passionate about ski mountaineering. For more information about his guiding, writing and photography check out his web site on: www.oconnoradventure.com

ALPINE SKI MOUNTAINEERING
VOLUME 1: WESTERN ALPS

by
Bill O'Connor

2 POLICE SQUARE, MILNTHORPE, CUMBRIA LA7 7PY
www.cicerone.co.uk

© Bill O'Connor 2002
ISBN 1 85284 373 X
A catalogue record for this book is available from the British Library.
Photos by the author, unless otherwise credited.

Dedication

To William Reed and Cameron Alexander

Acknowledgements

This guidebook is the product of more than three decades of enjoyment and good company in the mountains. To all those that have been my companions on these marvellous journeys I give a heartfelt thanks. Special mention has to be made of Sallie O'Connor, who has not only been my willing partner in the hills but has also had to put up with me pouring over maps, pictures and guidebooks at home during the writing of these volumes.

Thanks to Cathy Duval for help with translations. To Jeremy Whitehead for his excellent pictures on pages 64, 66, 67, 69, 71, 76, 79 and 80. His experience of skiing in the Haute Maurienne and Vanoise is vast. Thanks to friends and fellow mountain guides: Hugh Clarke for contributing the pictures on pages 106, 114 and 159, and Rob Collister for his pictures on pages 17 and 52.

Finally, I must thank the team at Cicerone for their hard work, and particularly Jonathan Williams for letting me realise my long-held ambition to produce guidebooks on Alpine ski mountaineering in English.

WARNING

Mountaineering can be a dangerous activity carrying a risk of personal injury or death. It should be undertaken only by those with a full understanding of the risks and with the training and experience to evaluate them. Mountaineers should be appropriately equipped for the routes undertaken. Whilst every care and effort has been taken in the preparation of this guide, the user should be aware that conditions, especially in winter, can be highly variable and can change quickly. Holds may become loose or fall off, rockfall can affect the character of a route, snow and avalanche conditions must be carefully considered. These can materially affect the seriousness of a climb, tour or expedition.

Therefore, except for any liability which cannot be excluded by law, neither Cicerone nor the author accepts liability for damage of any nature (including damage to property, personal injury or death) arising directly or indirectly from the information in this guide.

Front Cover: On the Schwartz Glacier below the Breithorn, looking towards the east face of the Matterhorn

CONTENTS

Advice to Readers

Readers are advised that while every effort is taken by the author to ensure the accuracy of this guidebook, changes can occur which may affect the contents. Glacier routes may change, and snow conditions influence which is the safest route. It is also advisable to check locally on transport, accommodation, shops, etc.

The author would welcome information on any updates and changes. Please send to: bill@oconnoradventure.com

SKI MOUNTAINEERING IN THE ALPS

Volume 1 – Western Alps
1 Écrins Haute Route
2 Haute Maurienne Traverse
3 Vanoise High-Level Circuit
4 Grand Paradiso Haute Route
5 Mont Blanc Haute Route
6 Mont Blanc High-Level Day-Tours
7 Classic Haute Route
8 Verbier High-Level Route
9 Arolla High-Level Circuit
10 Zermatt & Saas Fee
   4000ers

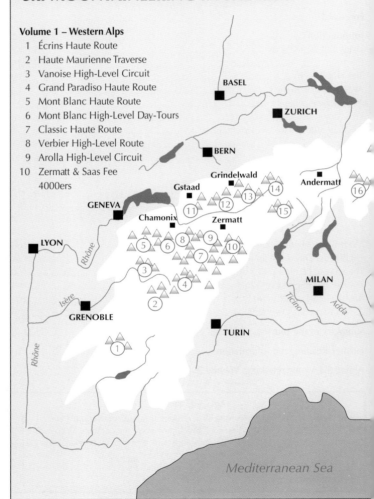

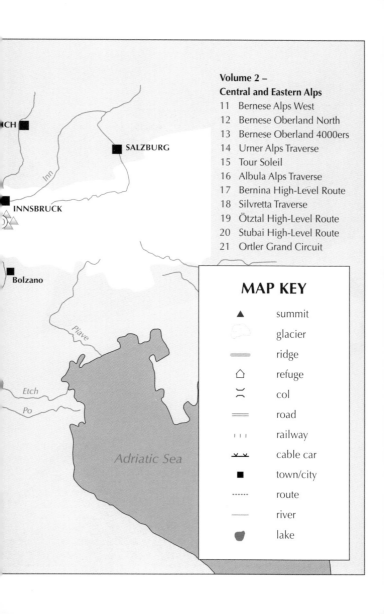

CH

SALZBURG

Inn

INNSBRUCK

Bolzano

Piave

Etch

Po

Adriatic Sea

MAP KEY

▲	summit
⬭	glacier
▬	ridge
⌂	refuge
⏝	col
═	road
⊦⊦⊦	railway
⊻⊻	cable car
■	town/city
······	route
—	river
⬤	lake

Skinning towards the Col Tour Noir with the Triolet in the distance

FOREWORD

After Fridtjof Nansen crossed Greenland at the end of the 19th century, his epic adventure provided the inspiration for many of the great ski journeys that followed. Although he was not a ski mountaineer his words, inspired by experience, capture the essence of ski travel: 'Is it such a deplorable fate to dash off like the wind...over a boundless expanse of ice... skis glid[ing] over the smooth surface so you scarcely know you are touching the earth? This is more, indeed, than anyone has any right to expect of life; it is a fairy tale from another world, from a life to come.'

There are few aspects of mountaineering as demanding and enjoyable as ski touring – it is not surprising, therefore, that it is becoming increasingly popular with skiers and mountaineers alike. As Sir Arnold Lunn, the father of Alpine ski racing observed: 'Ski-mountaineering is no mere variation of mountaineering. It is the result of the marriage of two great sports, mountaineering and skiing.'

The reasons for the increasing popularity of ski mountaineering appear obvious to those who have done it. Foremost, there seems to be a desire on the part of skiers to find adventure away from crowded slopes and well-groomed snow. One can find deep satisfaction in developing and displaying the skill, independence and effort needed to enjoy the hidden heart of mountains where solitude, beauty, adventure and sheer enjoyment prevail. Surely this is the perfect antidote to modern living. Also important has been the development of modern ski equipment and clothing. These have definitely made off-piste skiing and mountain touring both more enjoyable and potentially safer.

I have long been of the opinion that any mountaineer unable to travel freely and safely in the high mountains during the months they are under a blanket of snow, and that, by definition, means on skis, is really an incomplete mountaineer. It is worth remembering that the Alps are, more or less, snowbound from November to June, and those unable to ski are virtually excluded from their heart for all but three months of the summer Alpine season.

This guide contains a selection of alpine high-level ski routes. There are other Alpine ski-routes out there, scores of them. I've had to leave out the odd personal favourite from this selection and I've undoubtedly left out whole areas that offer superb touring. Perhaps the most deserving cases will one day appear in a third volume. The routes described can also be varied to make them longer, shorter or more or less demanding. The skier able to take on these challenges, though, should have no difficulty adapting the routes I've described to meet their ability and ambition.

As every writer knows, and as Arnold Lunn wisely wrote, 'Guidebooks merely describe the skeleton, leaving the memory to clothe it with romance.' That said, the mountain lover who completes these routes will, by any yardstick, have a comprehensive knowledge of the High Alps and can be regarded as a well travelled and complete Alpine ski mountaineer. Good touring.

Bill O'Connor
International Mountain and Ski Guide
Cumbria

The magnificent panorama of skiable 4000ers above Zermatt, including Lyskamm, Castor, Pollux and the Breithorn

10

INTRODUCTION

This guidebook is about 'high-level' ski routes, and includes a selection of my favourite tours. For most English-speaking skiers, there is probably only one high-level route – that between Mont Blanc and the Matterhorn, often called the Haute Route. Most people are astonished to learn that long before it was skied in 1911, it was a recognised high-level hike. In fact it had been established by members of the Alpine Club as a relatively quick, high-level crossing between the burgeoning villages of Zermatt and Chamonix. They called it the High Level Road. Today, this route between Chamonix and Zermatt is arguably the most famous

and sought-after ski tour in the world. It may therefore come as a surprise to the many who regard it as the one and only Haute Route that there are in fact a multitude of other worthwhile high-level routes throughout the Alps.

In reality, the Alps are criss-crossed with stunning ski tours, most being as sought after by knowledgeable skiers as the Chamonix–Zermatt High Level Route itself. Many have gained a classic status, though it is difficult to define what 'classic' means. It is certainly more than a matter of being popular. The skiing on a classic tour should, in my opinion, demand a range of skiing and

It doesn't get much better:
a perfect day on the Breithorn and Schwartztor Glacier above Zermatt

mountaineering skills, call for good navigation, and be challenging, but nevertheless remain logical as a ski tour. The need to carry skis should be an occasional and logical necessity only. Once completed a classic tour should provide a better understanding of an area's physical geography. And above all, however, it should be an enjoyable journey. Each tour in this book is arguably the best of its kind and standard in a particular mountain area and epitomises what is best about ski mountaineering in that region.

Unlike the famous Chamonix–Zermatt High Level Route, most of the tours recommended in this book did not originate as walking tours but were established as ski-touring itineraries. Because of this many offer far better downhill skiing than the famous Chamonix–Zermatt traverse! The problem for many English-speaking skiers has been finding out about all the other really great high-level routes – hence this two-volume guidebook.

The routes that follow represent a wide selection of tours throughout the Alps. If you linked them together you could traverse the Alps from the Dolomites, Tyrol and Bernina in the east to the Oberland, Pennines and Mont Blanc right down through the Grand Paradiso, Vanois and Dauphiné in the south. The Alps from end to end, just about.

Within the two volumes are included some of the finest, most

accessible Alpine ski tours in the world – only available, of course, to the complete mountaineer. The selection covers tours in the most important Alpine regions. They are also varied in length and difficulty, although most fit within a full week's touring. Of course, if poor weather or conditions prevail they can take a lot longer! The routes also include a mix of 'circular' tours, which are convenient for those wishing to leave car or equipment in one place, and 'linear' routes that journey hut to hut, even from country to country. These usually require a little more organisation with regard to logistics, travel and packing.

The routes described are all Alpine – in other words, they require both skiing and mountaineering skills. While technical climbing ability of a high standard is not essential, the skills required to operate on steep slopes and glacier terrain, where cramponing, ropework and crevasse rescue may be necessary, are essential for safety, as are navigational skills. It goes without saying that avalanche awareness skills and knowledge are vitally important for everyone who intends to ski mountaineer.

USING THIS GUIDEBOOK

Each tour section in this book follows the same pattern.

An **introduction** provides a little about the mountaineering history of the area and gives some background on both the Alpine area and the tour itself.

Skinning above Arolla with the stunning backdrop of Mont Collon and the Evêque beyond

To help simplify planning the following **information** is given at the start of each tour:

- start
- finish
- duration
- location
- difficulty
- best time for the tour
- facilities (accommodation and supplies)
- access
- maps.

This is followed by **route summary**, detailing the key place names found on the map for each stage of the route. This useful for plotting the route when used in conjunction with the recommended 1:25,000 maps.

The itinerary for each tour is broken down into recommended **day stages**. Each stage begins by giving details of:

- ascent
- descent
- principal aspect
- difficulty
- time.

This is followed by a description of the day's stage. Describing a ski route is very different from describing summer climbs or walking routes. In summer, paths and features are clear and often waymarked. During the ski season many features including way-markings, outcrops, streams and paths will be buried under snow. Therefore ski-route descriptions are less prescriptive – snow conditions and ability will often decide the precise line of ascent or descent. Some routes are obviously determined by the terrain – say when it follows a valley, ridge or couloir – but the precise line will always be a matter of judgement or of following old tracks! When crossing untracked snow, the skier will have to call on skill and judgement to find the best line through crevasses or to make the most efficient and safest track on a snow-laden slope. Even if you know an area in summer, don't assume the ski track will follow the same route. Although maps and route descriptions can indicate crevasses, their precise position changes with the movement of the ice. At all times the ski mountaineer must be willing to make a judgement about route choice and snow stability – no guidebook can do that. One of the great things about ski touring is, no matter how popular the tour, after new snow you will always have a clean sheet to work with. At all times the ski mountaineer must be observant, paying particular attention to the critical factors of weather, terrain and snow conditions before committing to a specific route.

Details of the routes are summarised in a table at the end of the book.

Route-finding

The length and difficulty of a day stage as given in the guide can be changed. You may think the day too short or the ascent of a particular peak too demanding. With a little care it is always possible to alter the route to suit your needs and the prevailing conditions to ensure the safest route.

If you decide not to follow the route exactly as described in the guide, you may be tempted to follow an existing ski track not yet filled in by fresh or windblown snow. Before following it, however, be in no doubt that the track is leading where you want to go. Many a skier has followed a trail carelessly only to arrive at the wrong col or summit! As a skier you have the option of making fresh tracks, both in ascent and descent, especially if the track in place takes a bad line or climbs inefficiently. It is satisfying to look back at a well-made track and know it is your own. On the descent, if too many tracks have trashed a fine slope it may be possible to make new ones, thus giving you the satisfaction of looking back at a set of cleanly carved turns – or not. Of course there is wisdom in following an established track through difficult terrain, say on a crevassed glacier or after heavy snowfall.

Late spring or early summer on the Weissmeis. Conditions remain good for a ski ascent

Maps and Diagrams

Accompanying each route description is a **route profile**, a diagram giving a clear indication of the ups and downs involved in each day's touring. Combined with the sketch map and description this should provide a useful impression of the rhythm of the day's stage.

The **sketch maps** of each tour will allow you to plan your route in conjunction with the route description and the recommended 1:25,000 or 1:50,000 maps. The sketch maps indicate cols, glaciers and significant spot heights mentioned in the text. They are not intended as a substitute for the recommended maps. They provide an indication of the route only.

For each tour a particular **map** or set of maps is recommended. Unfortunately several of the tours require numerous maps. Ideally use those at 1:25,000 scale. The Swiss, in conjunction with their National Ski Federation, have produced special ski maps at 1:50,000 scale. These have ski routes marked and also have a wealth of information about routes printed on the back of the map. These are very useful. For general planning 1:100,000 scale maps are recommended. Although useless for navigation, unless you are in a car, they are ideal for plotting the route and getting a feeling for the areas surrounding a given tour.

Huts and Other Useful Contacts

A list of addresses and telephone numbers for each tour, including the telephone numbers of the Alpine huts mentioned in the route, is given at the end of each tour. Specific details about huts have been included in the tour description where necessary. Also given at the end of each tour is contact information for tourist offices, police, rescue services and weather information.

ON TOUR

Always take time to consider the weather conditions, not just on the day you start but over the days and weeks before your tour. They will have an effect on the snowpack and your safety. The snowpack will, in turn, affect the difficulty of the route, the time a stage takes and the dangers that exist. No guidebook can cover all the variables. The descriptions are based on known routes done in stable conditions. Just occasionally conditions for a tour will be idyllic: perfect snow, few crevasses and a track in place, all of which will make for a direct route and a fast time. Much more likely is a varied mix of good and unskiable snow, blue sky and bad visibility, as well as easy or complex crevasse systems to negotiate. The key is to expect the unexpected and allow yourself time to deal with problems.

Remember, if you can't see the slope ahead, be it an icefall, cliff, couloir or valley, it is all but impossible to make an informed judgement about the dangers you face or to ski it safely. In these conditions the best option may well be to stay put in the

Sunshine and drifting snow make for a pretty picture, but signal a clear warning to the aware ski mountaineer

hut, read a book or practise a few rope skills nearby.

Times and Conditions

The time given in the guide for any particular stage is an average one for a party of reasonably fit skiers moving steadily and climbing at around 300m per hour. Where appropriate they provide generous timings, rather than assuming a fast pace. The times given cannot take into account problems arising from poor fitness, skiing ability, navigation or conditions. In the unlikely event that any of these apply to your party you will need to adjust the tour accordingly.

If you arrive at the Alps tired after travelling, and with no acclimatisation, the first few days may well feel tough. If you haven't toured for a year your equipment may feel unfamiliar –

and like your legs might not work very well! As a friend of mine says: 'Don't let your enthusiasm make appointments your legs and lungs can't keep!'

Once on tour most skiers find they acclimatise quickly and become more efficient and familiar with their kit. It takes a while to fall into the delightful rhythm of skinning, carrying a rucksack and, of course, hut life. After a while you are likely to find that the times given in the guide seem more generous. However, that's as it should be. Remember, having time in hand means having a safety margin should problems arise.

By late spring, when the days lengthen, it is normal to arrive back at the huts in the early afternoon with plenty of daylight left. It can feel as if half the day has been wasted. In fact it is often the case that the snow by

*Crevasse rescue techniques
need to be understood and
practised by everyone going on a glacier tour*

then is too soft or dangerous for enjoyable skiing. You can always spend the afternoon doing a transceiver search or crevasse rescue.

Remember, weather and snow can change rapidly on tour. A slope on which a party an hour or so ahead of you were able to make perfect linked turns may have become a nightmare by the time you come to descend it. It pays to plan ahead and think about slope aspect, weather conditions and timing.

Start Times

These vary throughout the season for the same route and will depend on a mixture of things: touring objective, party fitness, snow, weather conditions and, of course, the whim of the hut guardian. Most Alpine huts have a set breakfast period during the ski-

touring season. Find this out from the guardian on arrival at the hut and plan accordingly. If you want to leave early let the guardian know. If you are lucky he might put a flask and some food out for you. On popular tours like the Haute Route you will invariably be involved in a massed start in the morning, which is all but impossible to avoid. Once underway in the morning groups quickly disperse, invariably coming together at bottlenecks such as steep climbs or abseil descents. If you want to get away quickly in the morning you need to get packed and organised the night before and get down to breakfast quickly!

Route-Finding and Navigation

It goes without saying that a 1:25,000 scale map, compass and altimeter, and the ability to use them, are essential for accurate navigation when ski touring. More and more skiers are using a Global Positioning System (GPS), and many maps provide a useful table of GPS co-ordinates to help plot waymarks quickly. Of course all maps have a grid system. Whatever tools you have, make sure you are skilful in using them. It is also advisable to spend time studying the map – mental rehearsal combined with map memory is a great benefit once skiing.

Altimeter

When skiing it is unusual to be able follow a direct compass bearing. Occasionally, on a well-covered glacier such as the Grosser Aletsch, it is possible, but normally crevasses have to be avoided and turns are essential.

An altimeter when skiing is an indispensable piece of equipment for accurate navigation in poor visibility. Wristwatch-style altimeters that can be worn outside a jacket are particularly useful. They can be referred to whilst on the move without loss of time or rhythm. Trying to gauge your speed of descent when skiing in poor visibility is all but impossible. An altimeter will save the day and give your altitude, if not your exact position, on a particular slope. In addition, they act as a barometer, indicating pressure variation and therefore potential changes in the weather.

GPS

Global Positioning Systems are increasingly being used by skiers. They are not a substitute for good

A watery sunrise seen from near the Col Crête Seche

navigation, which is as much about good judgement and route choice as simply about knowing where you are. However, when combined with sound navigational skill they are very useful, and very reassuring in white-out conditions.

THE HUT SYSTEM

One of the benefits of skiing in the Alps is the extensive chain of Alpine mountain huts. The building of huts began early in the history of Alpinism, and they serve us well. Above all they make it possible to enjoy extensive ski touring without the need to carry heavy camping, cooking and sleeping equipment, or food; the combined weight of which, for a long tour, would make touring unbearable, if not impossible, for many skiers. Alpine huts have been built and are owned by various national Alpine clubs – namely the Swiss Alpine Club (CAS), French Alpine Club (CAF), Italian Alpine Club (CAI), Austrian Alpine Club (AAV) and German Alpine Club (DAV). Non-Alpine countries have contributed financially to some. There are also a growing number of private huts.

The huts are open to everyone, and usually offer unsegregated dormitory-style accommodation. However, members of an Alpine club or organisations affiliated to the UIAA (International Union of Alpine Associations) may have reciprocal rights giving them discounted bed-nights. Non-members simply pay a little more. The huts currently represent very good value. Most huts are open during the main season, usually mid-March until some time in May, during which time a hut warden is resident and can provide meals. At other times there is usually a small winter-room with mattresses, blankets and often a stove, fuel and a few cooking utensils.

Don't expect running water to be available at the huts during the ski season. Most use melted snow for water, and none is made available for washing. That said, a few do have water and even hot showers through-out the year.

Booking the Huts

It is recommended that you book your place at the hut in advance; this lets the guardian plan meals and accommodation properly. It also avoids gross overcrowding. Failure to do so can make for watery soup and worse! Guardians make a great effort to find everyone a place; you will rarely be turned away. However, some huts get very busy during the holidays, particularly over Easter on the more famous haute routes. If you change your plans and have made a booking, let the guardian know, so that your place can be made available to others. Guardians, if they are expecting you, may also be concerned about your non-arrival if you have failed to cancel your booking. Many skiers also phone ahead to let the guardian know

19

they are on their way. Most huts have radio-telephones, which you can use.

Meals

Many huts offer an almost restaurant-style service throughout the day, although both the breakfast and evening meal are normally set menus. Food at huts is not discounted to members of any Alpine club. Vegetarians should make a point of informing the guardian when they arrive at the hut because meat is the norm. Vegetarian options are limited – eggs, cheese and pasta head the list. Breakfast remains light in most huts, some say slight. It is certainly traditional: tea, coffee or hot chocolate with bread, butter, jam and sometimes a little cheese. A few huts have improved their breakfast offering by providing cereal and yoghurt.

Most huts sell sweets, chocolates and a small selection of food items. Some will provide a simple packed lunch – be sure to order it the night before and not during the morning rush.

Some huts allow self-catering, but you normally have to carry your own stove, fuel and utensils. Guardians will also cook simple food such as pasta and soup for you, charging a fee to do so. Understandably they don't always like doing it, especially if the hut is crowded, and you are likely to find yourself eating last.

Water

Water is an obvious problem during the ski season. There is plenty of snow

and ice, but hopefully it will remain frozen, which means that running water is in short supply. Hut water supplies have to be melted from snow and ice, or in some cases helicoptered to the huts. It comes as a surprise to many hut users that water has to be paid for and that during the ski season very few huts have running water for washing or lavatories. Be prepared to buy bottled water or have hot water or tea in your drinking bottle in the morning. Some guardians fill water bottles the evening before so that they can cool before morning. It is not uncommon to see them being taken to bed to serve as a hot-water bottle!

AVALANCHE AWARENESS

When people and snowy mountains meet the potential for avalanches exists. Every skier should make it their business to understand avalanche phenomena. They are not an act of God; in fact about 80% of avalanche victims trigger the avalanche they get caught in.

During a ski tour the risk of avalanche is a constant danger that must be faced whenever your skis are on the mountain. Assessing risk ultimately depends on your knowledge and the care you take in assessing the danger. The process doesn't need to be a lengthy one that will spoil a good day on the hill, but it does need to be a systematic one, both before and during a tour. A systematic approach will enable you to gather key information that will allow you to make an

Group under instruction during an avalanche awareness course

informed judgement about snow stability and avalanche hazard.

On tour, assessment of avalanche danger should be gained from gathering observed facts about the terrain, the snowpack, past and present weather, and from slope stability tests.

Ask yourself these questions:

- What information do I have that makes me think this slope is stable?
- What is the likely outcome for our group should the slope avalanche?
- Do we have an agreed emergency proceedure in place if it does?

THE HARD FACTS

Here are some hard avalanche facts based on Swiss statistics.

- Of skiers completely buried by an avalanche only 4 in 10 survive.
- Over a recent period 1347 people were known to have survived partial or complete burial by avalanche. Of these:
  - 39% dug themselves out
  - 34% were dug out by survivors on the scene
  - 27% were recovered by rescue teams – but most of these were near ski resorts.
- In that same period close to 1000 died – two-thirds by suffocation.

First, the good news is that, if the victim is alive after the initial impact, they have an 80% chance of survival if dug out in the first 12 minutes. But after that the news is not so good. It is thought that unless recovery is made within 30 minutes, an avalanche victim's chances of survival are less than 50/50.

The fact is that less than one-third of those buried survive, and this doesn't refer to deep burial. For those buried under less than 50cm of snow the survival rate is around 45%. At more than 2 metres only 1% survive, and below 3 metres…?

Best Practice

It is 'best practice' to:
- avoid obvious avalanche danger
- adopt safe procedures when travelling and, in the event of an avalanche, not to rely on others outside your group for rescue.

Rescue, if it is to be successful, must come from your own party, and **speed** is the all-important factor. Speed comes from planning, preparation and practice.

The Three Essentials

To maximise speed of rescue there are three 'must have' bits of equipment for every off-piste skier and ski tourer.

Transceiver – Owning one will not stop you getting caught in an avalanche, but if you are buried it is almost your only hope of being found – dead or alive. A transceiver is not a substitute for good practice, it is part of it. Route planning, route choice and constant avalanche awareness are the basic ways to minimise risk.

Every skier going off-piste or touring should have a transceiver. However, it is not enough to own one: you must wear it and know how to use it

Powder Hound carving a head plant!

in an emergency. That skill only comes from practice, regular and realistic practice against the clock – remember the first 12–15 minutes are all-important. Get into the habit of turning your transceiver on when you put it on in the morning and leaving it on until you return in the evening. Never turn your transceiver off during the day to save the battery. It is all too easy to forget to turn it on again.

Having turned your transceiver on make sure you carry out a transceiver check both on leaving the hut and at other times during the day, especially after rest stops. Rather than standing around in a huddle and checking transceivers work when you are standing next to each other, get one person to ski away (say 30m) from the group with their transceiver in receive mode. Then one at a time the group members with their transceivers in transmit mode ski towards the person on receive. As soon as the person receiving picks up a signal they should signify it. This gives a good indication of signal strength, which seems to vary amongst different makes of transceiver. Someone should then check that the person on receive is also transmitting correctly. Everyone should carry spare batteries on a long tour.

Snow shovel – It is not enough to have one or two shovels in a group of four or six skiers. Everyone should carry an avalanche shovel. One reason why I like touring with North American clients is the size of their shovels! They carry big metal-bladed things that can shift snow fast, not flimsy things the size of desert spoons. This really is a case of size being important. Don't bother with tiny blades that attach to ice axes or ski poles that bend the moment they come into contact with hard snow. If you were buried what would you want your rescuers to use? A JCB!

Avalanche probe – Used in conjunction with a transceiver avalanche probes can quickly establish the exact position of a body before initial digging. For a final search or deep burial they are a must.

They are also useful for testing the snow structure by probing rather than digging once you know the snow profile on a given aspect. This can be particularly useful when on the move.

Avalanche probes being used to confirm a snow profile on a slope where a snow-pit had been dug previously

But it is not enough simply to carry these essentail tools, you have to know how to use them in an emergency. Practise regularly.

AVALANCHE BULLETINS

There is a wide range of information that can be accessed via telephone, fax and the internet during the ski season. The following list covers the major Alpine areas described in this book and will help you gather information before and during a tour.

France

Telephone: Dial International Code (0033) followed by 89 26 81 020 and the department number:

Haute Savoie	74
Savoi	73
Isere	38
Hautes-Alpes	05
Alpes Haute-Provence	05 or 06
Alpes Maritime	06

Website: www.meteo.fr/temps/france/avalanches

Italy

Telephone: Dial International Code (0039) followed by (0461) 23 00 30. When phoning from outside Italy leave the 0 off the number in brackets (below):

Valle d'Aosta	www.regione.vda.it/bollnivometeo.nsf	(0165) 77 63 00
Piedmonte	www.regione.piemonte.it/meteo.neve.htm	(011) 318 55 55
Trentino	www.provincia.tn.it/csvdi.bolletino	(0461) 23 89 39
South Tirol	www.provincia.bz.it/valanghe	(0471) 27 11 77
Lombardia	www.regione.lombardia.itmeteonew.nsf/home/valanghe	
		(0478) 370 77
Veneto	www.arpa.veneteo.it/csvvdi/bolletino	(0436) 79221
Friuli-Venezia Giulia	www.regione.fvg.it/meteo/valanghe.htm	800 860 377
Meteomont service	www.meteomont.sail.it/meteo/neve/htm	

Austria

Telephone: Dial International Code (0043) followed by the number below.

Voralberg	www.voralberg.at/lawine	(05522) 1588
Salzburg	www.land-sbg.gv.at/lawinen	(0622) 1588
Oberosterreich	www.ooe.gv.at/lawinenwarndienst/	(0732) 1588
Tirol	www.larwine.at/tirol	(0512) 1588
Osttirol	www.larwine.at/tirol	(0512) 1588
Steiermark	www.larwine.at	(0316) 1588
Karnten	www.larwine.at	(0463) 1588

Switzerland
Dial International Code (0041) followed by number below.
All regions   www.slf.ch/avalanche/avalanche-de.html
                     www.slf.ch/avalanche/avalanche-fr.html
                     www.slf.ch/avalanche/avalanche-it.html   848 800 187

Assessing Snow Stability
There is a lot you can do to assess snow stability before you go on tour. Snowpack is the result of past snowfall and weather conditions, and you need this information to understand how it has built up. Weather reports, avalanche bulletins (see box p. 24) and web sites provide an often detailed picture of what conditions have been and are now like on the hill. Tourist Offices and Guides Bureaus, as well

SNOW STABILITY CHECKLIST			
Evaluation Factors	Record Information	Influence/Trend Stable	Unstable
Slope angle			
Snow depth			
Past avalanche activity			
Current avalanche activity			
Shear tests			
Snowpack structure			
Snow temperature			
Precipitation			
Wind			
Effect of past winds			
Surface penetration			
Air temperature			
Solar radiation			
Snow settlement			
Humidity			
Weather forecast			
Avalanche forecast			
Stability rating (based on the above)			

as knowledgeable locals, can all provide additional information.

Once on tour you need to evaluate snow stability constantly because the slope aspect, altitude and conditions are always changing. To some degree ski mountaineers gain a feel for slope angle, snow and conditions – it's called experience. I find it helps to have a procedure when evaluating

snow stability. Aim to gather targeted information that will help you build up an informed picture. Eliminate unessential information and go straight for the bull's-eye.

On p. 25 is a checklist for assessing snow stability similar to those used by British mountain guides and avalanche professionals around the world. I'm always surprised how easy

KEY POINTS IN AVALANCHE AWARENESS

- Understand what causes avalanches, and learn to recognise, test and record these causes.

- Understand weather and find out about past, present and future conditions that have and are likely to influence snow stability. Snowfall, wind and temperature all influence avalanche risk.

- Appreciate the significance of slope angle and aspect to avalanche risk. Slopes between 25° and 40° are perfect for skiing on, but they also present the greatest risk.

- Be observant. Conditions on tour change fast not only from day to day but from one slope to another and even on the same slope. Look for indicators of instability.

- Ensure you are properly equipped and clothed, and that equipment is all in good working order.

- Ensure you are prepared for emergencies and have a fast and efficient procedure in place to deal with them.

- Choose your route with care, and avoid suspect slopes. Be prepared to change or abandon your route. Be aware of the danger presented by slopes above and below the one you are on.

- If you have to travel through high-risk terrain do so with care. Be prepared at all times, make everyone aware of the risks and ensure they know what's expected of them in the event of an avalanche.

- Organise your party for maximum safety. If possible let people know your route. On hut-to-hut tours this is relatively easy, as you move between huts and guardians are expecting you. If you change your plan let the guardian know. Don't simply fail to turn up at a hut where you have booked a place.

it is to overlook obvious signs of both danger and stability. The checklist is useful as an *aide-mémoire* to help systematically observe, test and record pertinent information and so build up a profile of snow stability at a particular time and place. This information provides a more complete picture when the time comes to make a judgement about avalanche danger.

Obviously some techniques here depend on knowledge and skill. Snow profiling and various stability tests, including the shovel shear test and Reusch blocks, although quickly learned, require training in interpretation. Anyone committed to ski mountaineering would be well advised to attend some kind of avalanche awareness training course where they can learn these skills.

Stability tests need to be carried out regularly. Although they can seem like a chore they do not take a great deal of time and they provide essential information. Once armed with the information in the chart above the picture of snow stability becomes a lot clearer. It may not be perfect, but it is better than a piece of seaweed or the 'It must be stable because someone else has skied it' approach to avalanche risk assessment.

Having made an assessment you can then modify your route or procedures on tour to maximise safety.

European Avalanche Hazard Scale
The European Avalanche Hazard Scale has been adopted throughout the Alps and is commonly used in conjunction with snow and avalanche reports. Often the degree of hazard existing at a given time is shown simply as level on a scale of 1–5 without further explanation. Understanding what the numbers mean is essential when weather reports are in a language you may not fully understand, but where a synoptic chart clearly indicates the level of hazard. The chart on p. 28 provides a detailed explanation of the European Avalanche Hazard Scale.

AVALANCHE ACCIDENTS

What do you do if you get caught in an avalanche? The fact is that once an avalanche has been triggered, unless it really is minor it is almost impossible to do anything. Things happen very fast, and you need a fair amount

Snow profiling to gather information essential for avalanche risk assessment during a tour

	EUROPEAN AVALANCHE HAZARD SCALE		
Degree of Hazard	Snowpack stability	Avalanche probability	Effects on off-piste and back-country activities/recommendations
1 Low	The snowpack is generally well bonded and stable.	Triggering possible only with high additional loads** on a few steep extreme slopes. Only a few small natural avalanches possible.	Virtually no restrictions on off-piste and back-country ski and travel.
2 Moderate	The snowpack is moderately well bonded on some steep slopes, otherwise generally well bonded.	Triggering possible with high additional loads**, particularly on steep slopes indicated in the bulletin. Large natural avalanches not likely.	Generally favourable conditions. Routes should still be selected with care, especially on steep slopes of the aspect and altitude indicated.
3 Considerable	The snowpack is moderately to weakly bonded on many steep slopes.	Triggering possible sometimes even with low additional loads**. The bulletin may indicate many slopes which are particularly affected. In certain conditions, medium and occasionally large sized natural avalanches may occur.	Off-piste and back-country skiing and travel should only be carried out by experienced persons able to evaluate avalanche hazard. Steep slopes of the aspects and altitude indicated should be avoided.
4 High	The snowpack is weakly bonded in most places.	Triggering probable even with low additional loads** on many steep slopes. In some conditions, frequent medium or large sized natural avalanches are likely.	Off-piste and back-country skiing and travel should be restricted to low-angled slopes; areas at the bottom of slopes may be hazardous.
5 Very High	The snowpack is generally weakly bonded and largely unstable.	Numerous large natural avalanches are likely, even in moderately steep terrain.	No off-piste or back-country skiing or travel should be undertaken.

Explanations:
** Additional load
  High: Group of skiers, piste machine, avalanche blasting
  Low: Skier or walker
Aspect: Compass bearing directly down the slope

Natural: Without human assistance
Steep slopes: Slopes with an incline of more than 30°
Steep extreme slopes: Particularly unfavourable in terms of incline, terrain profile, proximity to ridge, smoothness of underlying ground surface.

of luck if you are caught in one. Call out to alert your companions and try to outrun it or ski off to the side of the avalanche if possible.

If you are caught:
- try to release your bindings
- release your ski poles
- try to stay on top of the snow by adopting a swimming or rolling motion
- before you are buried pull your knees up to your chest and cover your face in an attempt to create an air pocket
- if you can thrust a hand up and out of the snow do so
- try not to panic
- pray.

If you are looking on:
- keep an eye on the victim/s for as long as possible
- point and follow the victim with your finger until they are buried – it's easy to lose track of them in a mass of moving snow
- keep pointing until the position can be marked with a ski pole. This will speed up the search.

The Search
- Appoint a search leader.
- Stay calm.
- Assess the whole situation and ensure the safety of the rest of the party. Visually scour the avalanche to see if you can see the victim/s – they may re-emerge lower down the slope. They may

only be partially buried, in which case there's no need to instigate a transceiver search.
- Organise the search based on observed facts, number buried, vanishing points and terrain.
- Begin the search as soon as possible. Eyes and ears as well as transceivers should be used.
- Switch off transceivers not in use if it is safe to do so.
- Maintain a controlled search pattern. Don't give up – despite the statistics victims have been recovered alive after very long periods of burial. Ensure a total and thorough search of the area. The victim may not be in the obvious deposition zone.
- Alert rescue services. They may be needed to evacuate victims, give medical help or search.

Immediate Response To Victims
Adequate primary care requires correct training in first aid. Ideally everyone should have this.
- Free the head and chest of the buried victim as soon as possible.
- Ensure they can and are breathing.
- If not give artificial respiration (CPR). Continue resuscitation until medical help arrives.
- Lay the person down correctly.
- Treat injuries where possible.
- Protect from further loss of body heat.
- Continue to observe the victim for any change in status.
- Evacuate to safety if required.

Signalling to a helicopter: note the skier is kneeling in front of a large flat area, back to the wind, with arms raised in a Y

HELICOPTER RESCUE

If there is an accident on tour that requires rescue assistance, helicopter is the recommended option. When someone is injured speed and safety are paramount. Trying to carry out self-rescue with an improvised stretcher, especially over difficult terrain, is complicated and slow, and may well result in further injury. It is important to know how to carry out such a rescue and be proficient at it, but it is not the best option when helicopter rescue is possible.

Helicopters have their limits, however, and require safe conditions to carry out a rescue. Poor weather conditions will restrict their safe operational use. In poor visibility, strong winds, and in snowy or icy conditions they may not be able to operate. However, the pilots of rescue helicopters carry out some remarkable missions. They should only be called in for an emergency or forced evacuation – do not endanger their lives unecessarily.

Insurance

The cost of emergency rescue, medical treatment, and repatriation, if necessary, varies from country to country, and you will need appropriate insurance to ensure that you are adequately covered. The BMC (Tel. 0161 445 4747, www. thebmc.co.uk) and AAC (Tel. 01707 324835, www.hbinsurance.co.uk) both provide travel insurance: make sure it covers ski mountaineering, not simply piste skiing.

What Information Do Rescuers Require?

If possible write down your message before calling for rescue. The information you give needs to be accurate, precise and concise, and writing it down will ensure this. It should include:

- name of person in charge/communicating with rescue base
- your position with grid reference
- your telephone number if phoning from a mobile
- number of people involved
- the name of the person/s injured
- the nature of the accident/injuries
- specific casualty requirements if known
- weather conditions at the site of the accident, including wind speed, visibility, cloud level, precipitation, etc
- information on whether a helicopter landing at the site is possible.

No Help Required

Yes We Need Help

Red Flare or Fire

Square of Red Cloth

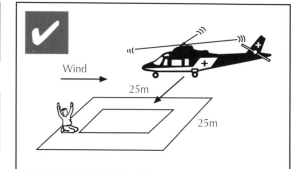
Wind
25m
25m

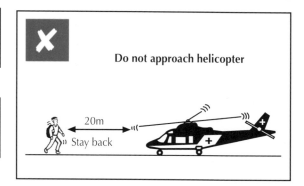
Do not approach helicopter
20m
Stay back

Distress signals and ideal layout for helicopter rescue

Safety Procedures On The Ground

- Never approach the helicopter when the rotor blade is moving.
- Do not approach the helicopter until told to do so by a member of the crew.
- Stay low or in a kneeling position with your back to the wind.
- Only approach the helicopter in the direction indicated by the pilot or crew member. It is usual to kneel up-wind, head on to the helicopter.
- Never approach from the rear of the machine or out of sight of the crew.
- Ensure that there is no loose equipment or clothing on the ground or on the person/s close to the helicopter.

The diagram on p. 31 page shows the ideal layout of the rescue site and the arm signals used to communicate with a helicopter.

In the mountains it is difficult to ensure flat ground. Remember a helicopter cannot land on steep slopes. It is important to stay below the pick-up area if the rescue is on a slope, since the helicopter may have to hover and winch the casualty aboard. The rotor blades may come very close to the slope above the rescue, so stay out of this zone. Stay below it and kneel.

Once inside the helicopter enjoy the view because it will be an expensive ride. Helicopter rescue is costly, so it is essential to have adequate insurance cover.

A SAFETY STRATEGY FOR SKI MOUNTAINEERING

As a mountain guide my own approach to safety is best summed up as the application of the three Ps: planning, preparation and practice. This may not be rocket science, but it is

Looking towards the deep cleft of the Col du Chardonnet between the Aiguilles Chardonnet (L) and Argentière (R) – seen from the Col du Grands Montets

certainly a combination of science, common sense and experience, which translates quite simply into 'best practice'.

Common Errors

Mountains can be dangerous – in winter and spring particularly so. But one of the great pleasures derived from ski mountaineering is the ability to journey safely over Alpine terrain that would be all but impossible without skis. Ski mountaineering accidents, alas, are all too frequent, with avalanches accounting for a high number of fatalities. By looking at the accident reports it is possible to identify a number of common errors (see box). Hopefully we can learn from these.

Planning and Preparation for your Ski Tour

There area lots of things you can do before a tour to help make it successful. Pre-trip planning is like a reconnaissance, and time spent on it is rarely if ever wasted. On p. 34 is a simple checklist which could form the basis of a pre-trip stategy.

COMMON ERRORS

- Wrong stability evaluation – in one study, over a five-year period, over 60% of avalanche fatalities were the result of wrong stability evaluation.

- Triggering the avalanche – most skiers caught in avalanches triggered the avalanche themselves.

- Taking uneccesary risks – in particular being on the wrong terrain and discounting evidence of snow instability that was contrary to what the skiers wanted to believe.

- Avalanching other members of the same group by triggering a slope above others.

- Failure to snow profile – weak layers that were easily triggered went undetected.

- Failure to identify dangerous accumulations of wind slab or appreciate the importance of past weather conditions.

- Triggering a small avalanche which in turn triggers a major slope failure. Failing to realise that in a snowpack of medium hardness large avalanches may occur.

- Triggering spontaneous and rapid release on sun-exposed slopes.

- Triggering a release from couloirs after small changes in temperature, wind or sun angle.

- Underestimating the power of a small slide – even small avalanches kill 42% of their victims.

PREPARING FOR YOUR SKI TOUR

Objective	**Decide on the route/ski tour/mountain**
Gather sources of information	Guidebooks, maps, articles and photographs all help build a mental picture of the tour. Tourist and Guides Offices are also sources of information.
Determine the terrain	Understand the terrain/slope angle. Is it rocky, glaciated, steep, couloir, forested, populated? Studying the terrain allows you to pre-empt problems.
Is it a known route or exploration?	Study the map carefully. Identify difficulties. Pre-empt problems. Don't assume a summer route is also the ski route.
How difficult is the tour likely to be?	Identify the specific difficulties/dangers. Does your party have the skill and fitness to handle the challenges?
Be properly equiped	What equipment is required for individuals and the group? Do you have it and can you use it? Can you repair it in an emergency?
Season and conditions	When is the best time of year for the tour? What effect will elevation and slope aspect have? How will these affect timing on the route? Being in the right place at the right time is often critical.
Weather/snow conditions – past, present and future	What have past weather conditions been? How have factors such as wind, precipitation and temperature affected the snow pack? What are the present conditions and what is forecast for the future?
Know what causes avalanches	Put snow and slopes together and the potential for avalanches exists. Learn about avalanche phenomena and the factors that contribute to avalanches.
Snow stability	How will poor weather and snow stability affect your options? Will you have route options or are you committed? Gather information about the snowpack from Guides offices, pisteurs, avalanche bulletins, personal tests.
Huts	Are there huts and are they open/wardened? If not, is the tour viable? Book accommodation in advance.
Contingency plans	What escape routes are possible once on tour? What alternatives exist in poor weather or dangerous snow conditions?
Emergency proceedures	Have information and a procedure in place relative to area of operation. Communications. Allow for the unexpected.

Once on tour it is important to remain alert, and there are many simple procedures that will make travel more efficient and improve group safety. A simple checklist will help you, but ultimately only practice will ensure that these procedures become second nature in the mountains.

Safety Strategy On Tour
A list of procedures that comprise a safety strategy is given in the box below. There is no sequential order to these procedures – they are ongoing and invariably overlap. The important thing is that they are understood and done. Use the box as a checklist.

	SAFETY STRATEGY ON TOUR
Equipment check	Ensure that you have all the equipment you need, that it works and is in order. Decide who carries what. First aid, repair kit, rope/s. What effect does this have on party organisation?
Make use of vantage points en-route	Take full advantage of spying out the route ahead and observing conditions and difficulties etc. Routes planned earlier may have to change in the light of new views and snow conditions.
Stay observent Gather information	Don't be afraid to ask hut wardens/guides and local experts for information. Stay alert. Take time to think about conditions and safety.
Effect of wind	Be observant. Look for the effects of wind. Cornices, slabs, drifting. How will it effect your route?
Avalanche activity	Be observant. Note old and new slides. What aspects and altitude as well as type. What affect will they have?
Hazards	Check out the route for unavoidable difficulties. What's the best option/route to overcome them?
Unseen hazards Terrain traps	Ensure that the route is not threatened from above or below by unseen/unnoticed dangers. Terrain traps.
Timings	In the light of conditions are the objectives and time available/allowed realistic?
Descents – think ahead	Should route be changed in the light of conditions during the ascent. Timing. Order of descent.
Options and escape routes	In the light of conditions will the route planned be possible? Can it be changed. What are the options?
Snow conditions Aspect	Are they as expected? Stability, quality. Does this affect safety? Are all aspects safe/dangerous.
Stability tests	Where and when to make them – if at all. If you feel unsure/unhappy about a slope ask yourself why? Check it out. Dig a pit and test your assumptions before you ski it.

There are other aspects of safety that relate to group organisation (see box).

GROUP ORGANISATION

- Assess the ability of every member of your group – who is the weakest link? Is the proposed tour more than they can deal with? Don't let ambition outdo ability.

- What safety measures and group organisation are needed for the tour, given the terrain and group size, ability, etc? How are you going to cross suspect slopes? How are you going to carry out avalanche procedures/tranceiver searches?

- Choose an able leader. Appoint a competent tail-end Charlie – not the slowest/poorest skier! Invariably the best skiers want to be up front putting in fresh tracks.

Putting in a Track

A good track is both efficient and safe in ascent and descent. A good route is not only safe, it should also be enjoyable skiing. It is not, however, always the shortest route, but should endeavour to:

- minimise exposure to terrain traps – dangerous places which would make the consequences of an avalanche or fall even more

serious (eg. traversing risky slopes above cliffs)

- minimise travel over slopes where snow stability is poor and the risk of avalanche suspected or known

- minimise kick turns, especially in exposed places where the consequences of a slip are serious

- minimise bunching together, especially in areas of suspect snow stability. Don't overload the slope.

Going uphill, a safe and efficient track should:
- avoid unneccesary kick turns, but not be too steep
- be within everyone's ability
- avoid cutting the slope above other members of the group
- ensure rests and regrouping occur only at safe locations
- use vantage points en route to plan and assess the route ahead
- allow observation of snow transportation and accumulation to help build a picture of snow stability.

Going downhill a controlled and disciplined descent allows you to:
- assess snow stability and be aware of changes casued by slope aspect, elevation and angle
- ensure that safety measures are in place to minimise the dangers to the maximum number of skiers within the group – speed and spacing are all-important

- communicate with all members of the group, and ensure all understand the hazards and what is required – have an agreed signal system
- maintain organisation and discipline and not let the descent become a free-for-all
- stick to your route or planned options – don't just 'go for it' into the unknown.

I began this section by mentioning the three Ps – planning, preparation and practice. Well, there should really be six Ps because – 'Planning, preparation and practice will prevent a poor performance!'

GRADING AND DIFFICULTY

There are several well-established systems used for grading ski mountaineering and off-piste skiing objectives. The Swiss, French, German, Italian and Austrian Alpine clubs have adopted these, or variations of them, for use in their guidebooks. Two widely used grading systems are the Blachère and Traynard scales, which are described below and have, more or less, been incorporated into this guidebook.

Blachère Scale

On tours where skiing rather than Alpine climbing skills are required the following adjectival grades are used.

BLANCHÈRE SCALE		
SM = skieur moyen MS = mittlere Skifahrer	Moderate skier	A skier of moderate ability capable of secure stem turns, off-piste, in all conditions, on slopes of 25–30°.
BS = bon skieur GS = gute Skifahrer	Good skier	Able to make controlled turns in all types of snow on slopes of 30–35°. Able to descend short steeper pitches and handle difficult snow.
TBS = très bon skieur SGS = sehr gute Skifahrer	Very good skier	Able to ascend and descend on skis sustained and exposed slopes that most people can only climb up with axe and crampons. These are slopes in excess of 45° requiring a high level of skill and experience, to say nothing of courage.

For ski-mountaineering objectives in high mountain and glaciated terrain where Alpine mountaineering skills are essential, the Blanchère scale uses the following grades.

BLANCHÈRE SCALE		
SAM = skieur alpiniste moyen **MAS = mittlere Alpineskifahrer**	*Moderate skier & Alpinist*	A skier of moderate ability capable of secure off-piste stem turns in all conditions on slopes of 25–30° but with sound basic mountaineering skills. These include good rope work and crevasse rescue, fall arrest and basic ability with axe and crampons in ascending and descending steep ground. Able to negotiate routes graded F and PD.
BSA=bon skieur alpiniste **GAS=gute Alpineskifahrer** *TBS=très bon skieur alpiniste*	*Good Skier & Alpinist*	Able to make controlled turns in all types of snow on slopes of 30–35°. Also able to descend short steeper pitches and ski in difficult snow. Must also have sound mountaineering skills listed above and be capable of negotiating more technical climbing terrain on routes graded AD and D.
SGAS=sehr gute Alpineskifahrer	*Very Good Skier & Alpinist*	Able to ascend and descend on sustained and exposed slopes that most people would climb with axe and crampons. These are slopes in excess of 45° requiring a high level of skiing and climbing skill – to say nothing of courage. Technical climbing D+ and above.

The Blanchère scale has been used in this guidebook. Invariably this means that the equipment carried must include rope, crampons, ice axe and the means to ensure safety on steep terrain and glaciers. This roughly relates to mountaineering grades as: SAM = F (facile); BSA = PD (peu difficile); TBS = AD (assez difficile). The mountaineering grades of D (difficile), TD (très difficile) and ED

(extrêment difficile) were not covered by the Blanchère scale and have traditionally been relegated to the realms of Extreme Skiing.

Traynard Scale
As the skier's ability to ascend and descend steep slopes has increased, the need has arisen for a more precise scale to highlight difficulty – the equivalent of the 'numerical grading'

Traversing the summit ridge of the Breithorn during a round of the Zermatt and Saas Fee 4000ers

given to rock climbs. The Traynard scale (see box) offers a way of highlighting a section of steep skiing. This is most useful within a tour where the general standard is suitable for someone with moderate Alpine and skiing ability (SAM), but where there is, for example, a short section S3 difficulty. A ski party may be capable of skiing S3 terrain but would prefer a more relaxed tour where the overall grade is less challenging, yet are prepared to ski a few steep sections. This scale allows for that specific difficulty to be recognised and highlighted.

TRAYNARD SCALE		
Grade	Angle of Slope	Description
S1		Well-defined, easy-angle tracks
S2		Easy-angled undulating slopes and hollows
S3	35°	Big slopes with low exposure. The ability to make controlled turns.
S4	45°	Big slopes with increasing exposure, or couloirs with limited turning space
S5	45–55°	The limit of possibility for even the good skier. Faces and couloirs.
S6	55°+	Slopes with great exposure and seriousness
S7	?	?

Using tensioned skis to provide a secure belay during a steep descent

It is essential to apply common sense when using this numerical scale, which quite reasonably is based on ideal snow conditions. On a good surface with stable conditions an S3 slope, 300m high, sounds inviting. However, the same slope in icy conditions is far less appealing, feels a lot steeper and can be quite daunting! Similarly a pitch or two of 40° skiing in a confined couloir can feel intimidating. My advice is, when using this scale, to consider the conditions and terrain and imagine how they will affect the slope and your skiing.

For pure climbing difficulty the established Alpine grading system using the following symbols has been adopted: F = easy; PD = not very difficult; AD = quite difficult; D = difficult; TD = very difficult; and ED = extremely difficult. This can be distinguished further by adding a + or – sign to the grade, giving PD+, AD-, etc. This grading system takes into account both the technical difficulty and overall seriousness of a climb and will be familiar to users of mountaineering guidebooks.

Thus a ski tour may be given a grade of: BSA. With the option of an AD+ ascent and involve sections of S3 steepness. Combined, these gradings hopefully provide the skier with a lot of useful information about the difficulty and demands of the route prior to setting out on tour.

EQUIPMENT LIST

This is the equipment list I use for my own ski tours. It is not a definitive list, but in my experience it covers the essentials for a hut-based, multi-day tour.

Given that you are not self-catering, your packed sack for a week-long ski tour, including your share of group equipment, should weigh between 8 and 12 kilos. Obviously there will be some variation in the weight and warmth of the clothing depending on whether you are touring early or late season and on anticipated weather conditions. If your sack weighs much more than indicated above, you need to take a close look at what you are carrying.

Personal Kit List
The Three Essentials
- **Shovel** – ideally a large metal-bladed shovel suitable for digging in hard snow.
- **Transceiver** – to be worn at all times when skiing. All transceivers should be a single-frequency 457kHz model. Some earlier models had a different frequency: avoid these. Take spare batteries.
- **Probe** – 2 metre minimum.

Clothing
- **Base layers** (x2) – one to wear and one spare. These should 'wick' moisture from your skin. Cotton is not a good base layer, since it absorbs moisture like a sponge and feels cold and clammy after a rest. Longjohns are a useful option early season.
- **Mid-layer** – Shirt or roll neck top.

Ideally this should also be light-weight and wicking.
- **Fleece jacket or sweater** – I use a Mountain Equipment Wind-stopper fleece. Highly versatile, it allows me to ventilate well but also offers protection in windy conditions when a shell jacket may not be appropriate. Some skiers prefer to carry two light-weight fleece pullovers.
- **Touring pants** – touring pants in a windproof stretch fabric are ideal. Available from a number of good Swiss manufacturers, or try Mountain Equipment's G2 pants or Stretchlite pants in the UK. They should be warm, and wind and snow proof. Some people are happy using stretch fleece pants under a light shell.
- **Shell jacket** – lightweight gore-tex is ideal, offering protection against the elements. For touring I like a fully functional attached hood that provides both protection and good visibility and I use a Mountain Equipment Paclite Jacket.
- **Shell pants** – either lightweight gore-tex or another breathable fabric. If you opt not to use touring pants but instead prefer technical shell pants worn over fleece pants, then I would opt for full-zip zipped gore-tex pants with braces. These can then be zipped on and off even over skis. Because I use touring pants I carry only very lightweight full

side-zipped shell pants (Mountain Equipment Drilite Pants) for emergency use only.

- **Socks** (x2) – one pair to wear and one pair spare. With well-fitting ski mountaineering boots you need only wear one pair of socks.
- **Ski gloves** (x2) – I carry one pair technical ski gloves plus a lighter windproof fleece pair. Make sure gloves are not too tight fitting. Hands tend to swell when skiing, and when wet they are difficult to push inside tight gloves. Loose linings are also a bad idea, as they generally pull out when you take the gloves off and are difficult to refit.
- **Sun hat** – ideally with neck protection – this is particularly important later in the season when the sun's strength can be enervating.
- **Warm hat** – ideally this should protect ears and side of face, and stay on in windy conditions.
- **Neck/ear band**.
- **Lightweight down vest or jacket** – (optional). These are ideal for sitting around cold huts or simply to pull on during a rest or lunch break. They weigh little, and in the case of an emergency can make all the difference. My favourite is the Mountain Equipment Lightline or Dewline Duvet.

Hardware

- **Skis** – I prefer medium stiffness all-terrain skis with a wideish tip

(circa 110) and a reasonable amount of side-cut offering a relatively short radius turn of about 20–22m. Wide, short and light seems to be the way to go.
- **Touring binding** – I currently use the Fritschi Diamir binding, as they offer great performance and ease of use. There are others available, and those wishing to go very lightweight should look at Dynafit Tourlite bindings. I like to have ski stops fitted and to carry safety straps.
- **Harscheisen** – removable crampons for your skis. They are usually specific to a given binding. It is possible to get by without them, but on icy mornings and for hard snow they save time and energy and increase safety.
- **Skins** – I prefer stick-on skins with a toe and tail attachment. If you change to fatter skis you should also change your skins for optimum climbing performance. You can buy skins custom shaped to fit carving-style skis. Make sure you have a stuff-bag to carry them in, and ensure you keep them clean and sticky.
- **Ski poles** – with powder baskets. I prefer one-piece poles, but two- or three-section poles are OK and pack away easily.
- **Ski mountaineering boots** – these should have a full climbing sole. Whatever boots you get they need to be comfortable for hiking on skis. I use Scarpa Denali,

which although not the lightest on the market offer a high level of performance as a ski boot yet remain comfortable for walking.

- **Custom liners** – these provide optimum fit and performance if fitted correctly. I use them for ski touring.
- **Custom footbeds** – correctly fitted, they offer optimum comfort and performance. Most boots are supplied with relatively poor quality footbeds as standard.
- **Rucksack** – 45–60 litre with waistbelt and side attachments for carrying skis. Get a sack that holds all you intend to carry. Try not to have much attached to the outside apart from skis, ice axe and possibly a shovel – the risk of loosing things, especially in a fall is high.
- **Water bottle/Thermos flask/ hydration system** – 1 litre minimum. If you opt for a hydration system ensure that the tube is insulated against cold, as they have a tendency to freeze up, leaving you unable to hydrate!
- **Mountaineering harness** – this should be large enough to fit over shell clothing and, ideally, have fully adjustable leg loops. Some skiers like a full body harness, but I feel the disadvantages outweigh the benefits. With a modern sit-harness inverting in a crevasse fall whilst carrying a rucksack is unlikely, especially when wearing skis.

- **Lightweight headtorch** – plus batteries and spare bulb.
- **Ice axe** – this should be suitable for self-arrest, belaying and whatever climbing the tour involves. Many lightweight axes are unsuitable for belaying and climbing but are ideal for self-arrest and ski races.
- **Crampons** – that fit your ski boots. Clip-on variety are ideal. Once again, choose crampons that suit the route. Many aluminum models, although lightweight and suitable for walking on snowy slopes, are unsuitable for climbing or hard snow, ice or mixed conditons.
- **Ski/mountaineering sun glasses** – high quality sunglasses that provide protection from light reflected off snow.
- **Ski goggles** – essential in poor conditions to provide full cover from wind-blown snow and ice particles.
- **Sunscreen** with high factor (20+).
- **Lip cream**.

Improvised Rescue Equipment

It is advisable that all members of a party to have the basic equipment to carry out crevasse or self-rescue – and know how to use it.

- Prusik loops (x3) – essential for glacier travel. As well as prusik loops there are various mechanical jamming devices available for improvised rescue. All require specific techniques and practice if they are to work efficiently.

- Lightweight pulley – essential for efficient improvised crevasse rescue.
- Screw gate karabiners (x4).
- Nylon belay slings (x2).
- Ice screws (x2).

Stuff

- Spare batteries for transceiver/camera.
- Small washkit/toothbrush/paste/wet wipes.
- Emergency food – a couple of high-calorie bars.
- Personal first aid – Elastoplasts and painkillers as well as prescription drugs, if required. It is essential to be able to carry out on the spot treatment in case of cuts and blisters.
- Toilet paper.
- Small washkit/toothbrush/toothpaste/wet wipes.
- Passport (for some tours).
- Alpine Club Card or reciprocal rights card.
- Money.
- Camera and film (optional).

Group Equipment

These items should be shared out and carried by members of the party.

- Group first aid kit – in addition to small personal first aid kit.
- Bivouac shelter.
- Spare ski stick.
- Radio/telephone.
- Altimeter – having more than one in a party is ideal.
- Spare skin.
- Compasses/GPS – It is advisable to have at least two compasses on tour.
- Maps.
- Ropes – 2x30m for most tours unless the route involves specific requirements (for example, if there are several 50m abseils you will require 2x50m ropes).
- Repair kit – for skis and bindings, etc.
- Stove – (optional) the ability to heat water and food can sometimes be useful in an emergency.
- Sleeping bag – (optional) a lightweight zipped sleeping bag for emergency use in case of an accident.

ÉCRINS HAUTE ROUTE

Though this rugged expanse of the Alps has long been popular with summer mountaineers, perhaps surprisingly it remains less well travelled by ski tourers, although La Grave and the surrounding area is rightly becoming a Mecca for dedicated off-piste skiers and ice climbers.

Although most English-speaking mountaineers know this region of the Alps as the Dauphiné, the French generally call it the Massif des Écrins, whilst a few locals still regard it as l'Oisans, a Roman name for a Celtic tribe, the Iceni, who once lived in the Romanche valley. During the French Revolution the Dauphiné was split into three regions – Isère, Haute Alps and Drôme.

The first ascent, in 1864, of the Barre des Écrins by Edward Whymper and A.W. Moore, and the later ascent of the magnificent Meije, ensured the Écrins had a place in Alpine history. This, the most westerly branch of the Alps, in fact boasts two summits over the magical 4000m mark, although in reality they are two parts of a single mountain. However, having a 4000er has established a summer pilgrimage trail to these most southerly of the Alpine giants. In the ski season, access is altogether more difficult and the summer hoard absent.

The Massif des Écrins is located south and west of the Cols du Galibier and Lautaret and west of the Guisane and upper Durance valleys and is wholly in

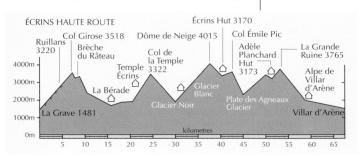

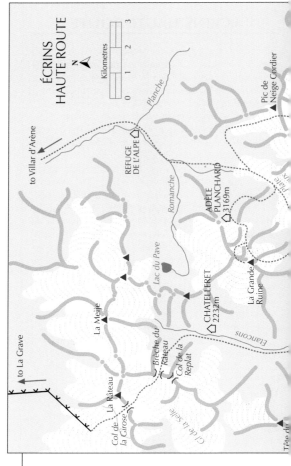

France. The massif forms a compact and complex, almost circular, block of mountains some 35km in diameter. The region is one of the most mountainous in the Alps. As well as the two 4000m tops there are eight other peaks over 3800m and at least 34 over 3500m. In fact

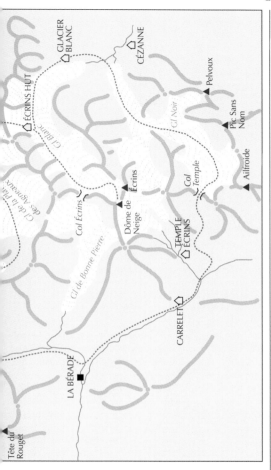

the area boasts over 100 summits above 3000m. The huge rock and ice walls of mountains like the Meije 3983m, Ailefroide 3954m, Pelvoux 3946m and Pic Sans Nom 3914m have all played a considerable part in Alpine history.

Despite its obvious mountaineering attractions and long history of tourism the area retains a sense of wildness. A single big resort town, the equivalent of Chamonix or Zermatt, right in the heart of the mountains does not exist. Although Briançon is a very fine city, the highest in Europe and the regional capital, it doesn't impinge on the mountains but stands apart. However, the absence of mechanical uplift around the main peaks means that the area has not seen the kind of development found in other resort areas. The region does boast famous ski towns such as Briançon, l'Alp d'Huez, Les Deux Alps and Sèrre Chevalier, but these are on the fringes of the main mountain areas, where their impact seems minimal. The village of La Grave remains an Alpine hamlet sheltering under the mighty Meije and has not developed into a 'normal' ski resort. Wisely, in my opinion, this stunning ski domain has been given over to off-piste powder hounds rather than corduroy cowboys. The minimal mechanical impact and building mean that skis are really the only efficient way to travel through the Écrins in winter. There was a great deal of resistance to the building of the lift above La Grave in 1976, so much so that a short while after it opened it was blown up!

The potential for ski mountaineering in the Massif des Écrins is huge, although at first glance touring routes are not obvious. The area is complex and rocky and the climbs often long, but so, consequently, are the descents. The Écrins is certainly not a soft-touch ski-touring area. The touring feels committing and customarily requires a complete range of skiing and mountaineering skills. Potential ski routes connect the many valleys which radiate from the region's centre, usually finding a way over narrow cols or snowy ridges; steep terrain and interesting route-finding are the order of the day, so that confident navigation is an advantage. Summits, where skiable, often involve cramponing and ropework, and abseils are not uncommon. In fact, the ski mountaineering is perfectly complete. As elsewhere in the Alps there are plenty of mountain huts, however one must be prepared for them to be unguarded – which in turn means greater preparation and heavier packs. On the other hand, the rewards are manifold. The itinerary in this chapter offers outstanding touring amongst magnificent mountains where the likelihood of solitude is high, certainly when compared to skiing in other parts of the Western Alps. The Dôme des Écrins, the most southerly Alpine 4000er, is likely to be the focus of most other skiers' attention.

The ski tour described lies wholly within the Écrins National Park, which was established in 1973; it is a circular route, beginning and ending in La Grave. This tiny village is a hospitable place well versed in the ways of mountaineers. La Grave offers over 7000 vertical feet of skiing in terrain that is dedicated to the off-piste and knowledgeable skier. Unlike most resorts the slopes are not groomed, there are no boundary ropes, no avalanche control, no closed signs and no ski patrol. In fact, it is the ideal place to warm up before starting a tour. Although small, La Grave offers plenty of friendly accommodation, has a local store and café. It also has, rather surprisingly, a modern ski lift to propel you into the high mountains at the start of the tour.

Although this is a strenuous and demanding route and feels committing, there are several points at which escape is possible, although returning to La Grave is far from convenient. There are escape routes from La

Ski mountaineering combines the skills of both skier and climber: here an abseil descent provides access to perfect powder and untracked snow

Bérarde, by regular bus via Bourg d'Oisans to La Grave, and also from the Refuge des Écrins to Ailefroide and then by bus to La Grave via l'Argentière-la-Besée, Briançon and the Col du Lautaret.

The Tour

Start:	La Grave
Finish:	Villar d'Arène – then by taxi to La Grave
Duration:	6 days touring
Location:	Wholly within France and the Massif des Écrins National Park
Difficulty:	BSA. AD. A strenuous and demanding tour in a wild setting that has a very remote feel. The tour requires good mountaineering as well as skiing skills. The route, however, is escapable and the summits are optional.
Best Time:	Mid-March to May
Facilities:	La Grave has a range of comfortable and friendly hotels, pensions, cafes and equipment stores.
Access:	Although La Grave is on the RN91 it feels off the beaten track and is accessible by local bus service, private car and taxi. There is no rail link. Grenoble is the nearest airport, although both Lyon and Geneva have good connections. La Grave is 77km from Grenoble, and the bus takes approximately 1h 45mins. The route from Briançon, over the Col du Lautaret, is often closed by snow in winter.
Maps:	IGN Meije–Pelvoux 1:25,000 Top 25 2436 ET. Didier Richard Écrins–Haute-Dauphiné 1:50,000

ROUTE SUMMARY

Stage 1: La Grave, 1481m – Gare des Ruillans, 3220m – Col de la Girose, 3518m – Glacier de la Girose, approx 3135m – Brêche du Rateau, 3235m – La Bérade, 1711m

Stage 2: La Bérarde 1713m – Refuge Temple Écrins, 2410m. Optional ascent to the Col des Avalanches 3499m.

Stage 3: Refuge Temple Écrins – Col de la Temple, 3322m – Refuge Cézanne, 1874m – Refuge du Glacier Blanc, 2550m

Stage 4: Refuge du Glacier Blanc – Dôme de Neige des

Écrins, 4015m – Refuge des Écrins, 3170m
Stage 5 : Refuge des Écrins – Col Émile Pic, 3491m – Glacier
de la Plate des Agneaux – Refuge Adèle Planchard, 3173m
Stage 6: Refuge Adèle Planchard – Grande Ruine, 3765m –
Villar d'Arène, 1650m

ROUTE ITINERARY
Stage 1
La Grave, 1481m – Gare des Ruillans, 3220m – Col de la
Girose, 3518m – Glacier de la Girose, approx 3135m –
Brèche du Râteau, 3235m – La Bérarde, 1711m

Ascent:	2120m (1720m by cablecar!)
Descent:	1904m
Difficulty:	PD+. A ski mountaineer's day involving an abseil descent of a steep couloir S3 and some splendid touring in a remote setting dominated by the La Meije.
Principal Aspect:	NW in ascent. S, E, S.
Time:	4–6 hours

The Écrins is not a region of the Alps spoilt by mechanical uplift, so the start of this tour offers a rare moment, one that will be savoured by some and scorned by others. If this is the first day of your tour, the 1700m of steep ascent from La Grave that the lift saves are well worth the expense. It will also make this a reasonable first day, especially as, at the end of the day, the metres skied in descent will greatly exceed the metres climbed.

Little prepares you for the fast ascent out of the gloom of the valley from the tiny hamlet of La Grave. At the top of the uplift the landscape is at once wild and austere. The magnificent north face of La Meije towers above the wild off-piste pleasures this area holds.

Once at the Gare des Ruillans, a short descent S leads to the Glacier de la Girose. A gentle ascent follows to reach the rounded, ice-capped Col de Girose, 3514m. The ascent passes S of a small serac barrier en route to the col and provides little more than a warm-up for what lies ahead.

To the S of the col a steep couloir, pitch of S3, leads to the Glacier de la Selle. The conditions in the couloir obviously vary; it has been skied, but an abseil or rope-protected descent is usual. Abseil anchors can be found on the rocks at the side of the couloir. Ability and snow conditions will determine at what point it is prudent to descend on skis to arrive on the relatively flat Girose glacier. Once on the glacier traverse SE to the foot of a gully, which which leads steeply upwards for about 100m to the Brèche du Râteau, 3236m.

The hard work for the day is now behind you. Descend eastwards over delightful slopes leading to the dramatic Val d'Etancons, which in turn gives access to the remote mountain village of La Bérarde. The descent of over 1000m to La Bérarde is a splendid one in a remote setting, all the while dominated by the magnificent south face of La Meije and La Grande Ruine. It is possible to break the descent and spend a night at the Refuge du Chatelleret, but that would disrupt the descent illogically, especially in favourable snow and weather conditions. On the other hand, those who scorned the ski lift may well be wilting at this point!

En route from La Berarde to the Temple des Écrins, with the peak of Les Bans in the distance

Stage 2

La Bérarde, 1713m – Refuge Temple Écrins, 2410m.
Optional ascent to the Col des Avalanches, 3499m.

Ascent:	700m, with an additional 1089m of ascent to the Col des Avalanches
Descent:	1089m if the ascent is made to the Col des Avalanches
Difficulty:	F. An easy day as far as the hut, after which there is the option of a splendid AD-ascent in the afternoon, which should only be undertaken if snow conditions are favourable.
Principal Aspect:	W
Time:	3 hours to the Refuge Temple Écrins and a further 3 hours to the Col des Avalanches

The route leads deeper into the remote heart of the Écrins by following the Val Vénéon SE over gentle slopes that in summer are verdant pastures. In winter the route follows the river's E bank, traversing numerous thought-provoking avalanche cones to reach the Refuge du Carrelet, 1909m. The route continues over the Plan du Carrelet to a point where the steep Vallon de la Pilatte enters the main valley from the NE. Begin climbing the steep slopes of the Abri du Carrelet, often made difficult by bushes if the snowpack is shallow, and so after a 400m ascent reach the Temple Écrins Hut, 2410m. The slopes leading to the hut present a known avalanche risk. In a year of heavy snow the hut is often completely buried and may have to be excavated. ▶

Stage 3

Refuge Temple Écrins – Col de la Temple, 3322m – Refuge Cézanne, 1874m – Refuge du Glacier Blanc, 2550m

Col des Avalanches

The option of a further ascent to the Col des Avalanches is available to those with spare energy. Not a name to fill a skier with confidence, but nevertheless a good tour. From the hut ascend NE towards the Pic Coolidge to reach the southern arm of the Glacier du Vallon de la Pilatte. Ascend this, steeply, towards the huge south face of the Barre des Écrins. Pass close to the rocks of le Fitre before turning E to reach the rocks of the Col des Avalanches, 3499m. Descend by the same route. Care needs to be taken on the steep slopes below the col.

Ascent:	1588m
Descent:	1448m
Principal Aspect:	SW, W in ascent. S, E in descent.
Difficulty:	PD+. The descent from the col is steep and is often best completed on foot.
Time:	6–7 hours

This stage has all the ingredients of a great mountain day – one that snakes its way through the wild mountainous heart of the Écrins massif and requires all the skills of a competent ski mountaineer for a successful crossing. You will be surrounded by high mountains, cross a remote col and descend a vast glacier-filled trench below some of the most impressive and severe north faces in the Alps. Total bliss! Local record has it that a *curé* from Vallouise once crossed the Col de la Temple to attend a service in La Bérarde and, what's more, he returned home the same day!

Climb SE from the hut, ascending steep, rocky snow- and ice-covered slopes and a steep snow runnel that finds a weakness around the SW spur of the Pic Coolidge. This first slope feels steep and exposed, and is best climbed on foot. A rope may well be required. Above this first abrupt step, gentler (albeit still unrelenting) slopes lead towards the small Glacier de la Temple. Ascend these NE to reach the northern branch of the Glacier de la Temple. Ascend this diagonally SE to reach the magnificently positioned Col de la Temple, 3321m. The col is an important crossing point on the ridge linking the Barre des Écrins with the Ailefroide – it provides access between the Vallouise and Veneon valley. The view from the col is stunning; in front of you the 1000m high northern flanks of the Ailfroide, Pic Sans Nom and Pelvoux are paraded above the deep trench of the Glacier Noir.

Traverse E from the col along a spur projecting into the Glacier Noir (bivouac box) in the direction of pt.3132m before descending the steep S-facing slope to reach the upper Glacier Noir at c.2900m. Several couloirs are possible, all offering a reasonable, albeit steep descent of this slope. Depending on conditions and route choice you may have to take your skis off to descend an arête and couloir on foot.

Having reached the glacier continue NE, keeping to the true left bank until pt.2540m, where the main glacier swings E. Cross to the N bank and descend this, aiming eventually to reach a point marked as a Site Glaciologigue, pt.1908m. From here it is possible to descend easily to the Refuge Cézanne, 1874m, and escape down the Vallouise.

From pt.1908m climb steeply N to reach the snout of the Glacier Blanc, 2267m. Under fresh snow cover the rocks steps can prove quite difficult. Traverse to the E side of the glacier and ascend a trough at the edge of the ice and continue the ascent until a final steep gully leads to the Refuge du Glacier Blanc, 2542m, superbly positioned to view the formidable bulk of Mont Pelvoux, 3932m.

Stage 4
Refuge du Glacier Blanc – Dôme de Neige des Écrins, 4015m – Refuge des Écrins, 3170m

Ascent:	1465m
Descent:	845m
Principal Aspect:	The main ascent/descent is N facing.
Difficulty:	PD-. High altitude and serious glacier terrain make this a magnificent mountain day. AD if the Barre des Écrins is climbed.
Time:	6–7 hours

This is a 4000m-summit day. In fact there are two summits over 4000m. The Barre des Écrins, 4102m, which is the most southern of the Alpine 4000ers, and its lower summit, the Dôme de Neige des Écrins, 4015m, which is the highpoint of this tour.

Aim to leave the hut early and begin by climbing the gentle moraine ridge N of the hut, staying well to

Looking towards the Barre des Écrins across the Glacier Blanc – the route traverses from R to L beneath the obvious seracs barriers. Dôme de Neige is the lower summit on the right.

the side of the glacier and its icefall. Gain the glacier above the icefall where the ice surface flattens out and travel becomes easy.

Stay on the N bank of the glacier, following it towards the Refuge des Écrins, staying on this bank of the glacier as it bends around towards the imposing north face of the Barre des Écrins, 4102m.

Continue across the almost flat surface of the glacier in the direction of the Col des Écrins. The route of ascent looks increasingly impressive as you skin closer to the Barre des Écrins; it appears to be a labyrinth of crevasses and seracs. But the ascent, although high, is relatively straightforward. The key is to avoid the two potentially dangerous areas of icefall. At first begin the ascent of the face close to the rocks of the Clochetons de Bonne Pierre. Continue the ascent diagonally leftwards (SE) towards the large bergschrund below the upper wall of the Barre des Écrins. At c.3761m turn back right (SW) climbing more gently to c.3850m, from where it is possible to traverse almost horizontally towards the Dôme de Neige des Écrins. The final climb, especially the bergschrund, can be awkward, sometimes difficult. From the summit the plethora of wild peaks that adorn l'Oisans is stunning, making this a real highpoint of the tour in every respect.

All that remains is the descent, and what a descent! A combination of altitude and attitude routinely provides good snow conditions for this magnificent ski. Once back on the flatter glacier, retrace your route to below the hut before making the final steep climb to the Refuge des Écrins, 3170m.

Stage 5

Refuge des Écrins – Col Émile Pic, 3491m – Glacier de la Plate des Agneaux – Refuge Adèle Planchard, 3173m

Ascent:	1191m
Descent:	1200m
Principal Aspect:	S, N, E
Difficulty:	A demanding day over steep and serious glacier terrain. No more difficult than what has gone before, but in an increasingly remote setting. Good visibility is essential.
Time:	4–5 hours

From the hut traverse diagonally NE to reach the tiny glacier tongue leading steeply to the Col Émile Pic, 3483m.

On the N side of the col the Glacier des Agneaux falls away steeply, which in good conditions and with good visibility offers a wonderful descent. Keep more or less to the true right bank. If the snow is thin lower down, leave the glacier going R at *c*.2900 and climb down on foot to reach easier ground. The valley falls steeply W towards the Glacier de la Plate des Agneaux. Descend these wonderful slopes and reach the glacier at *c*.2237m.

From this point it is possible to descend N to Valfourche, the Refuge de l'Alpe and finish the tour in La Grave.

The proposed route turns S and ascends the Glacier de la Plate des Agneaux on its N bank to gain its upper basin at *c*.2850m. At this point turn N, climbing steeply to reach the narrow Glacier de la Casse Deserte, which is climbed in the direction of La Grande Ruine. At the

Traversing below the seracs on the Barre des Écrins

head of this glacier, on the right, cross the Col des Neige, 3348m, to reach the Glacier Supérieur des Agneaux. Climb N for about 100m towards the rock spur descending from the Roche Meane before making your descent to the unwardened Refuge Adèle Planchard.

Stage 6
Refuge Adèle Planchard – Grande Ruine, 3765m – Villar d'Arène, 1650m

Ascent:	592m
Descent:	2115m
Principal Aspect:	E, S
Difficulty:	PD
Time:	2–3 hours in ascent

The final day of this Écrins Haute Route involves an ascent of the Grande Ruine and is a fitting finale to a magnificent tour. Although not an obvious ski peak, a narrow glacier on the east flank of the Grande Ruine holds the key to its ascent. In fact this is more or less the route of the first ascent of the mountain, which was made by those eccentric Alpine pioneers W.A.B. Coolidge and his aunt Mlle. Brevoort, with their guides Christian Almer senior, Peter Michael junior, Christian Roth and Peter Bleur on 19th July 1873.

From the hut retrace the descent route from the previous day, crossing the spur of the Roche Meane to reach the W branch of the Glacier Supérieur des Agneaux. Ascend this, initially in the direction of the Col du Diable, before curving left towards the Breche Giroud-Lezin, 3666m, and then in the direction of the NE flank of the Grande Ruine, climbing as far as the bergschrund. It is normal to make a ski depot at this point. Now climb steeply to reach the east ridge, follow this in an exposed position to the Pointe Brevoort 3765m, the S and main summit of the Grande Ruine. This is a most magnificent vantage point, regarded by many as the finest in the Écrins massif.

Descend as far as the hut by the route of ascent. From the hut, if snow conditions allow, it is possible to make a steep descent southwards directly to the Glacier de la Plate des Agneaux. It is essential to have stable snow conditions for this descent.

The start of another perfect day in paradise

There is an alternative descent to the Glacier de la Plate des Agneaux, which is to retrace the route of ascent via the Col des Neiges and the Glacier de la Casse Deserte.

Once on the Glacier de la Plate des Agneaux, turn N and descend the glacier and its valley to reach the Pont de Valfourche, 2048m. Turn NE and descend the valley of the nascent Romanche along its right bank before making a short ascent to the Refuge de l'Alpe, 2077m, above the confluence with the Chamoissiere. Continue down the Romanche valley and reach, with a bit of polling and walking, Villar d'Arène, 1650m, from where a bus or taxi will ferry you the remaining 3km to the fleshpots of La Grave! In Roman times Villar d'Arène acted as a staging post between Italy and Roman Gaul.

ÉCRINS HAUTE ROUTE: USEFUL INFORMATION

Huts

Centre Alpin in La Bérarde, 1720m. Tel: 76 79 53 83

Refuge de Temple Écrins, Tel: 04 76 79 08 28

Refuge du Glacier Blanc, 2550m. Tel: 92 45 44 07

Refuge des Écrins, 3170m. Tel: 92 45 24 52

Refuge Adèle Planchard, 3173m. Tel: 76 44 75 94

Alpes de Villar d'Arène, 2077m. Tel: 92 24 45 04

Useful Contacts

La Grave Tourist Office. Tel: 76.79.90.05

Isère Department of Tourism. Tel: 76 54 34 36

Écrins National Park. Tel: 92 51 40 71

La Grave cable car. Tel: 76.79.91.09

Weather Information

Haute Alpes. Tel: 08 36 68 02 05

Grenoble. Tel: 36.65.02.38

Briançon Meteo. Tel: 92 21 10 42 Tel: 36.65.02.05

Isère. Tel: 08 36 68 02 38

Emergency and Rescue

Police emergency. Tel: 122

La Grave rescue. Tel : 76.79.91.02

PGHM de Briançon. Tel: 04 92 21 07 58

PGHM de Grenoble. Tel: 04 76 77 57 70

General emergency number for area CRS/PGHM. Tel: 04 92 22 22 22

HAUTE MAURIENNE TRAVERSE

This is an excellent, relatively short tour, which traverses the impressive southern section of the Central Frontier range of the Graian Alps. The Haute Maurienne remains a well-kept secret to most English-speaking skiers, despite being first-class touring terrain. This ski-mountaineering morsel should give you an appetite to further explore this delightful area.

The Central Frontier range of the Graians follows the Franco-Italian border for a distance of 85km and includes a plethora of peaks over 3500m. This route, through an area known locally as the Haute Maurienne, explores only a short segment of the southern section of the Central Frontier range. For French skiers it is fast becoming a classic, although it remains little known to others: its lack of that seemingly essential ingredient, a 4000er, has undoubtedly made it a no-go area for tourers who, engrossed in ticking 'Alpine giants', rarely venture beyond the Grand Paradiso. This is a delightful route which, if all the summits are climbed, demands skiing and mountaineering skill in equal measure. Even without the summits it remains a varied and interesting route in a wild setting. That said, there are several escape possibilities should poor weather or conditions prevail.

The ascent of the L'Albaron, 3637m, is in every way the high point of the tour, offering magnificent views

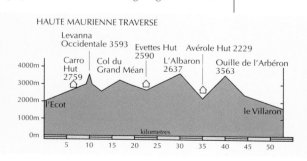

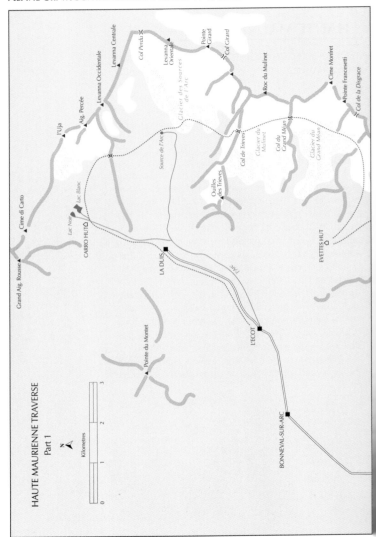

HAUTE MAURIENNE TRAVERSE
Part 1

Kilometres

0   1   2   3

N

Grand Aig. Rousse

Cime di Carto

L'Uja

Aig. Percée

Levanna Occidentale

Levanna Centrale

Col Perdu

Levanna Orientale

Pointe Girard

Col Girard

Roc du Mulinet

Cime Monfret

Pointe Francesetti

Col de la Disgrace

Glacier des Sources de l'Arc

Source de l'Arc

Lac Blanc

Lac Noir

CARRO HUT

Ouilles des Trièves

Col de Trièves

Glacier du Mulinet

Col du Grand Mean

Glacier du Grand Mean

EVETTES HUT

LA DUIS

L'Arc

L'ECOT

Pointe du Montet

BONNEVAL-SUR-ARC

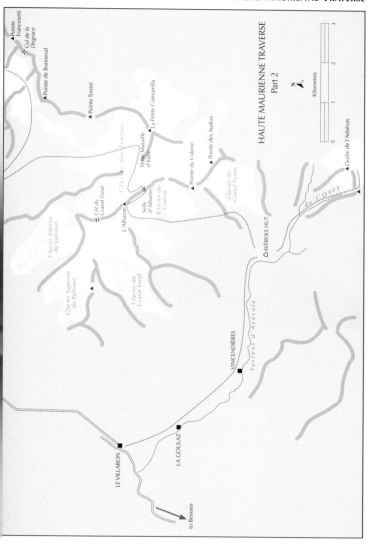

HAUTE MAURIENNE TRAVERSE
Part 2

Kilometres

0   1   2   3

N

Pointe Francesetti
Col de la Disgrâce
Pointe de Bonneval
Pointe Tonini
La Petite Ciamarella
Petite Muraille d'Italie
Glacier des Sarettes
Col du Grand Fond
Glacier Intérior du Vallonet
L'Albaron
Selle d'Albaron
Glacier du Colerin
Pointe du Colerin
Pointe des Audras
Glacier des Grand Pareis
Glacier Superior du Vallonet
Glacier du Grand Fond
Ouille de l'Arbéron
Vallon d'Oney
AVÉROLE HUT
VINCENDIÈRES
Torrent d'Avérole
LE VILLARON
LA GOUAZ
to Bessans

amid splendid glacier scenery. Technically two key passages open up the route: the crossing of the Col du Trieve and the Selle de l'Albaron.

Although the huts on this tour are normally guarded during the spring touring season, it is essential to phone both for a reservation and to make sure that the guardian will be in place to provide meals. When unguarded the huts remain open. However, you will need to carry and cook your own meals. Blankets, cooking utensils and wood are provided. It may be advisable to carry a lightweight gas cooker.

Tourers resting on the Selle de l'Albaron, 3474m

Optional Start from Val d'Isère

By starting out of bounds, as it were, in Val d'Isère, an enjoyable two-day extension to the Haute Maurienne route can be had. It begins with an initial warm-up day ascending Pointe Pers or Col Pers using the lift system, followed by a descent to the Prariond Hut. From there an interesting traverse over the Col du Montet leads to Carro Hut, with the possibility of an ascent of the Grand Aiguille Rousse. The only problem is that any equipment left in Val d'Isère has to be retrieved at the end of the tour, which finishes in the Arc valley. While the route by road back to Val d'Isère is a long one, there is a fairly direct route back on skis over a snowed-up Col de l'Iseran from Bonneval.

The Tour

Start:		Bonneval-sur-Arc
Finish:		le Villaron
Duration:		4 days
Location:		SE corner of the Vanoise National Park E of the Arc valley between the Col de l'Iseran and Col du Mt Cenis following the Central Frontier range of the Graians along the Franco-Italian border
Difficulty:		SAM. Several PD ascent options with short S3 pitches.
Best Time:		February–May
Facilities:		Chalet Bonneval sur Arc, Tel: 04 79 05 83 78. Open all year. If you are intending to stay in Bonneval this is a good base from which to begin the tour.
Access:	*By air:*	Lyon, Geneva, Grenoble are all reasonably close. There are train connections to Modane.
	By road:	Take the A43 Auroroute: Grenoble–Chambéry–Turin. Leave at Modane. RN6 in Modane at Lanslebourg. D902 in Lanslebourg to Bonneval. From Modane there is a shuttle bus to Bonneval-sur-Arc.
	By train:	Trains to Modane, some 4 hours from Paris by TGV.
Maps:		IGN 2633 ET Top 25 Tignes–Val d'Isère–Haute Maurienne

ROUTE SUMMARY

Stage 1: Bonneval-sur-Arc, 1790m – Carro Hut, 2759m

Stage 2: Carro Hut, 2759m – Levanna Occidentale, 3593m – Col du Grand Méan, 3214m – Evettes Hut, 2590m

Stage 3: Evettes Hut, 2590m – L'Albaron, 2637m – Refuge d'Avérole

Stage 4: Avérole Hut, 2229m – Ouille de l'Arbéron – le Villaron

ROUTE ITINERARY

Stage 1

Bonneval-sur-Arc 1790m – Carro Refuge 2759m

The steep slopes above the Arc and beneath the Ouille de Gontiere present avalanche risk, so be sure to find

Ascent:	969m
Difficulty:	Straightforward ascent. Steep in places. Stable snow conditions are essential for this ascent.
Principal Aspect:	E, S
Time:	3 hours

The magnificently positioned Carro Hut, 2759m, with the Grand Aiguille Rousse and Cime du Carro

out about snow conditions before leaving.

If the road from Bonneval to l'Ecot and Le Mollard is open, it is possible to take a taxi and save an hour on the ascent. Below l'Ecot, cross to the NW bank of the Arc valley and climb this. Stay on this side, traversing beneath the cable car (not for skiers) and continue following the valley to Tuliere and la Duis, 2145m, where the main valley turns E. Continue climbing N, more steeply now, traversing above the Lechans stream to the Carro hut.

Stage 2

Refuge Carro, 2759m – Levanna Occidentale, 3593m – Col du Grand Méan, 3214m – Refuge Evettes, 2590m

Ascent:	1248m including the Levanna summit
Descent:	1417m including the Levanna summit
Difficulty:	Levanna Occidentale is PD+ with a short section of S3.
Principal Aspect:	W, S
Time:	5–6 hours

This is a magnificent day spent traversing the western flank of the impressive mountain ridge that forms the Franco-Italian frontier. It provides an interesting route meandering amid unspoilt glaciers in a wild and remote setting. With an early start, it is possible to include the summit of the Levanna Occidental, 3593m.

Leave the Carro Hut and go E, traversing S of Lac Blanc and all the while climbing steadily to the Col des Pariotes, 3034m. From the col you get a good view of the route to the Levanna Occidental. Climb E to gain the gentle Glacier de Derrière les Lacs at pt.3091m and ascend to a band of crags at c.3350m, where the slope above steepens. If snow conditions are favourable, it is possible to continue on skis up the west flank and then on foot along the north-west ridge to the summit. The views from the summit into Italy are extensive. Descend to the Col des Pariotes, 3050m, by the route of ascent.

From the col descend SE into the valley of the Arc to reach its source at c.2750m. Continue S across open slopes to reach the edge of the Glacier des Sources de l'Arc, close to the Lac des Sources Inferieures. Continue S, climbing more steeply towards the Col de Trieves.

Looking towards the notorious Col de Trièves (slab avalanche) with the Mulinet

The climb to the col is abrupt and a key section of the route. Reach a steep ramp under a well-marked slanting rockface. Follow this ramp to the Col de Trieves. Now continue E up the ridge for 100m, and then cross S on the gentle slopes of the Glacier du Mulinet to the Col du Grand Méan, 3214m. After the steep climb to reach the col, the glacier, with its broad and gentle slopes, provides a sharp contrast to the jagged rock peaks of the main ridge.

Having reached the Col du Grand Méan the main difficulties are now past and the descent can begin. Drop W below the rocky south face of the Point du Grand Méan until it is possible to turn S to gain the gentler slopes of the Glacier du Grand Méan below pt.3154m. Contour the glacier without losing too much height, traversing below the west ridge of the Pointe Francesetti, 3425m, and so gain the southern bay of the Glacier du Grand Méan at c.3050m. Turn W and descend to the Plan des Evettes following the main valley to pt.3502m. At its northern end climb steeply to the Evettes Refuge above the Lacs des Pareis. ◀

On the traverse of the Glacier du Grand Méan it is possible to make a detour and ascend the Pointe Francesetti by climbing directly up the southern edge of its W flank. Although quite steep, it is without technical difficulty. The ascent adds about 1h 30mins.

Stage 3

Evettes Refuge – L'Albaron, 2637m – Refuge d'Avérole, 2229m

Ascent:	1047m
Descent:	1408m
Difficulty:	PD+. SAM
Principal Aspect:	N, NE in ascent. S, W in descent.
Time:	5–6 hours

A day of interesting route-finding through magnificent glaciers and seracs with the added spice of an ascent of l'Albaron, 2637m, which was first climbed in 1866. This mountain provides a really fine descent.

From the hut, descend a short way to the Plan des Evettes and cross the wide melt-water plain to the S. Go

Traversing the Plan des Evettes towards the Evettes Glacier and La Petite Ciamarella, 3549m

in the direction of the Glacier des Evettes, which drapes the northern flank of the Petite Ciamarella, 2549m. Ascend the true right bank (E) of the ice tongue, finding a way through the serac barrier between 2750m and 2850m, usually without much difficulty, to gain the flatter glacier above. Now go in the direction of the Petite Muraille d'Italie, W of the Cimarella's summit. The glacier steepens dramatically at *c*.2946m. Climb to *c*.3050m before bearing W towards l'Albaron. Ascending in a wide arc traverse under the rockwall and skirt around its right-hand end to follow a glacier ramp back L, above the rockwall, before continuing steeply to the Selle de l'Albaron, 3474m, a well-defined depression on the south-east ridge of l'Albaron.

Now the work really begins! The ascent of the ridge awaits you, and in places this involves scrambling, although it offers no great difficulty. You will need to carry your skis. The highest point of l'Albaron's ill-defined summit can be found at its northern corner, which incidentally is also the start of the descent.

From the summit descend W for 100m, then turn S at *c*.3500m, descending steeply to the edge of the Glacier du Colerin at 3091m.

At this stage, it is possible to continue the descent and end the tour by following the valley of the Torrent d'Avérole W to the hamlets of Avérole and Vincendières. In a good season, you may be able to ski further, possibly to la Goulaz, and so reach le Villaron in the main Arc valley.

A descent to this point can be made from the Selle de l'Albaron for those not wishing to go to the summit.

From *c.*3100m continue traversing S, aiming towards pt.2946m. Descend steeply at first, and then at *c.*2800m traverse E around a crest to descend steeply once again. Go towards the Ruisseau du Veilet before turning SW, following a broad hollow to the Refuge d'Avérole, 2229m. This provides a fine descent. ◀

Stage 4
Refuge d'Avérole, 2229m – Ouille de l'Arbéron – le Villaron, 1733m

Ascent:	1334m
Descent:	1713m to Vincendières
Difficulty:	PD+. The S-facing slopes can quickly clear of snow later in the season.
Principal Aspect:	S, NW
Time:	6 hours round trip hut to summit.

This is a fine summit with which to finish the tour, although it is not a climb for novices. From the wild setting of the refuge cross SE to the Val d'Arnes and then follow the Risseau de l'Oney, staying below the well-defined rock face beneath the Crete de la Valletaz that runs parallel with the stream. Climb steeply in several places to reach the small Glacier d'Arbéron. Ascend this as far as the Col de l'Arbéron, 3022m. From the col the Ouille de l'Arbéron throws down its west-southwest ridge. Follow this to the summit. It is possible to gain the summit on skis, but it is more usual to crampon up the last section. Descend by the same route. Alternatively the north-west face provides a more difficult ski descent option.

From the refuge, the descent follows the valley of the Torrent d'Avérole W to the hamlets of Avérole, 1990m, and Vincendières, 1850m. In a good season, you may be able to ski further, possibly to la Goulaz, 1760m, and so reach le Villaron, 1733m, in the main Arc valley.

View of the south flank of l'Albaron, 3474m

HAUTE MAURIENNE HAUTE ROUTE: USEFUL INFORMATION

Huts

Carro Refuge, 2759m.
Tel: 04 79 05 95 79.
Guarded in spring. 24 places.

Evettes Refuge, 2590m.
Tel: 04 79 05 96 64.
Guarded in spring. 20 places.

Avérole Refuge, 2210m.
Tel: 04 79 05 96 70. Guarded 20
March–27 May. 30 places.

Useful Contacts

Bonneval-sur-Arc Tourist Office
Tel: 04.79.05.95.95;
Fax: 04.79.05.86.87
E-mail: info@bonneval-sur-
arc.com

Weather Information

Savoie. Tel: 08 36 68 02 73
Isère. Tel: 08 36 68 02 38

Emergency and Rescue

Police emergency. Tel: 112

Emergency number for Maurienne
area CRS/PGHM.
Tel: 04 79 05 11 88

CRS Modane. Tel: 04 79 05 11 88

PGHM de Modane.
Tel: 04 79 05 50 98

LA POULÉ – VANOISE HIGH-LEVEL CIRCUIT

At first glance 'The chicken' may seem a strange, slightly disrespectful name for the Vanoise National Park, especially when you discover that it was established in 1963 and was the first national park to be recognized in France. But the name, given to the park by locals, makes perfect sense – not because, as some have suggested, chicken is the main dish on the *menu touristique*, but because the shape of the park's outline clearly resembles this noble fowl! Not convinced? Then take a look at the front of Les Trois Vallées map (3534 OT), and I think you'll agree – La Poulé is quite proper.

The mountains and glaciers of Massif de la Vanoise, which rise between the Isère to the east and the Arc to the south, dominate the park. These are sometimes referred to as the western Graian Alps. Tarentaise, the old Roman name for the region, is also widely used. The highpoint of the Vanoise is the Grande Casse (3852m), a fine mountain that stands amid a plethora of peaks, of which no less than 107 rise above 3000m. Despite the vast number of ski installations and hideous concrete structures that service parts of this, the largest ski domain

LA POULÉ – VANOISE HIGH-LEVEL CIRCUIT Stages 1–5

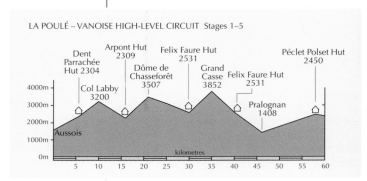

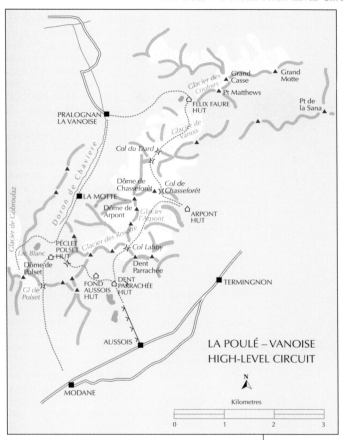

in the world, it remains a charming place with pockets
of authenticity, traditional villages, abundant wildlife
and rich forest.

For some reason this veritable ski-touring paradise is
often overlooked in favour of the higher Grand Paradiso,
Pennine Alps and Oberland. To give perspective to this
often bypassed touring area it is worth recalling that the

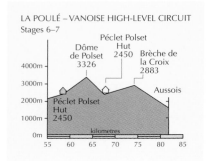

LA POULÉ – VANOISE HIGH-LEVEL CIRCUIT
Stages 6–7

mountains and glaciers of the Vanoise, some 12km long, are the second largest glacier and snowfield system of their kind in the Alps. Above all, they retain a sense remoteness and inaccessibility that makes them the ideal preserve of the ski mountaineer.

The route described below doesn't follow a frontier or mountain ridge, instead it is a circular tour from Aussois. Pralognan, a still largely unspoilt village, is also a good starting point and may be more convenient for some. If this is the case, then it is simply a matter or rearranging the tour slightly. The benefit of a circular tour is its convenience for those arriving by car and those wishing to leave luggage at the point of departure.

Aussois, at the foot of the Dent Parrachée, is a busy ski resort easily reached by road transport or rail. Modane, a few kilometres down the Arc valley, is the main rail terminus, and local buses connect both resorts. Accommodation is plentiful in both Modane and Aussois.

The mountain huts in the Vanoise are worth a mention. They belong to either the national park, the French Alpine Club or are private. They are not always guarded either in summer or winter, so it is advisable to phone before arrival to make reservations. There is a central reservations system in operation which might prove useful (Tel: 04 79 08 71 49). When unguarded, all the huts remain open for use. They have blankets, usually a store of wood for the stove, and they all have cooking utensils. When guarded the wardens can generally provide a cooked meal. If you are self catering you would be advised to carry a gas cooker and fuel – just in case.

The Tour

Start:	Aussois, 1483m. An alternative start from Pralognan is also possible.
Finish:	Aussois, 1483m, or Pralognan, if used as the starting point.
Duration:	6–7 days if the option to climb the Grande Casse is taken.
Location:	The Vanoise National Park – France
Difficulty:	SAM. The Grande Casse offers a more difficult (D) and very worthwhile option, in which case the grade of the tour is BSA.
Best Time:	March–April
Facilities:	Modane and Aussois have a wide range of accommodation, and the usual supermarkets and stores associated with busy ski resorts.
Access:	Aussois is less than 2 hours drive from airports at Lyon, Geneva, Chambery and Torino. By train Aussois is 7km from the main station at Modane. Using the TGV Modane is 4 hours from Paris. Throughout the year express trains such as the Paris–Milan or Lyon–Milan stop at Modane. By road access is easy via the A43 or A41 from Geneva, Lyon and Valence, exiting at Modane–Haute Maurienne Vanoise and then via the N6 to Modane and D125 to Aussois. Depending on snow conditions, access is possible via Mont Cenis, Iseran and Galibier Cols.
Maps:	IGN Les Trois Vallées 3534 OT Top 25

ROUTE SUMMARY

Stage 1: Aussois to the Refuge Dent de la Parrachée
Stage 2: Refuge Dent de la Parrachée – Col du Labby – Refuge de l'Arpont, 2309m
Stage 3: Refuge de l'Arpont, 2309m – Dôme de la Chasseforêt, 3507m – Refuge du Col de la Vanoise (Felix Faure Hut), 2531m
Stage 4: Optional. The Grande Casse, 3852m, SW flank from the Refuge du Col de la Vanoise (Felix Faure Hut), 2516m

Stage 4 or 5: Refuge du Col de la Vanoise (Felix Faure Hut), 2531m, to Refuge de Péclet Polset, 2450m

Stage 6: Refuge de Péclet Polset, 2450m – Dôme de Polset, 3326m – Refuge de Péclet Polset, 2450m

Stage 7: Refuge de Péclet Polset, 2450m, to Modane or Aussois

ROUTE ITINERARY
Stage 1
Aussois to the Refuge Dent de la Parrachée

Ascent:	1061m from Aussois
Descent:	300m from Plan Sec lift
Difficulty:	A short day that can be combined with piste skiing or a very late start.
Principal Aspect:	W, S
Time:	3 hours or 45 minutes (with ski lift)

Climbing the final few metres to the Dent de la Parrachée Hut

Only an absolute purist would disdain to use the ski lift to reach the high point of the Plan de Sec and from there descend to La Fournache, from where an easy climb of 45 minutes leads to the hut. With such a short day it is

possible to combine it with a day's skiing. Those not using the lift system will reach the refuge in about 3 hours.

Stage 2
Refuge Dent de la Parrachée – Col du Labby – Refuge de l'Arpont, 2309m

Ascent:	817m
Descent:	1019m
Difficulty:	SAM. Crevasse danger. Short steep section before the col. Careful navigation required to find the hut
Principal Aspect:	W, N, NE, E
Time:	2hrs 45mins–3hours to Col du Labby; 4–5 hours total

Good visibility is required to make this crossing, as the best line and the hut are not easy to find. Although these are not massive summits, the terrain is glaciated and at times complicated, although not technically difficult.

From the hut climb N in the hollow of a shallow re-entrant before ascending steeper slopes towards the Plan de la Gorma, *c.*2760m. Continue up open terrain towards the Lac Genepy, 2906m, passing it on its W bank. Continue climbing towards the Roche Chevriere, avoiding the steeper slopes on the right by moving to the left (W) in a broad sweep before returning right (E) to reach the foot of the Glacier Labby at *c.*3000m. Trend E at first, towards the Col du Moine, then at *c.*3200m bear N towards the obvious Col de Labby, crossing a steep gully and so reach the col. The col offers a marvellous panorama which includes the north face of the Dent du Parrachée, Dômes du Genepy and the Arpont.

Descend NE from the col past a rock island. Below this, pass through a gap (*c.*3150m) in the rock ridge that descends NE from the col, and so gain the E branch of the Glacier de la Mahure. ▶

Descend the crevassed Mahure glacier northwards below the impressive north flank of the Dent Parrachée, crossing it at a flattish area at *c.*2850m to reach pt.2814m – an area of open slopes off the glacier to the

Alternative Route via the Col du Moine, 3228m
This offers similar difficulties to the Col du Labby and allows the E branch of the Glacier de la Mahure to be reached more directly. Instead of turning N at *c.*3200m continue directly E to the Col du Moine. On the far side descend the Glacier de la Mahure directly. Some crevasse danger.

N. Make a gently descending traverse to the NE, staying below a ridge to reach a shoulder at c.2750m. Traverse the shoulder N around the ridge to gain the Glacier de l'Arpont on its far side. Now continue the traverse across the glacier staying above (W) Lac de l'Arpont to reach slopes on its N side. Continue the descent E in a hollow that soon becomes the bed of the Ruisseau de l'Ile. The well-concealed hut can be found on the lateral moraine of the l'Arpont glacier to the left.

Stage 3
Refuge de l'Arpont, 2309m – Dôme de la Chasseforêt, 3507m – Refuge du Col de la Vanoise (Felix Faure Hut), 2531m

Ascent:	1456m
Descent:	1238m
Difficulty:	SAM. Mainly route-finding through glacial terrain. A key stage on the crossing of the Vanoise glacier.
Principal Aspect:	E,S,N
Time:	6–7 hours

Begin by retracing your tracks to the flattish area on the Glacier de l'Arpont above the Lac de l'Arpont. Continue W up steep, crevassed slopes beneath the Dôme de l'Arpont to reach another flattish area at c.3100m below a zone of crevasses and seracs. At this point turn N and continue climbing the broken section of glacier to reach the easier slopes of the upper glacier plateau E of the Dôme des Nants. Continue more easily to the summit ridge of the Dôme de Chasseforêt, 3586m.

From the summit descend W along the broad summit ridge to the Col de Chasseforêt, 3507m, and then turn N on the Glacier de la Vanoise towards the Dôme des Sonnailles. At c.3360m bear NNE and descend to the Col du Pelve, 2992m. Continue N, making a short climb to the Point Ouest du Mont Pelve, 3254m. Continue by making a descending traverse N before turning E below the Pointe du Dard at c.3100m. If possible try to maintain height; this will then leave a short climb to gain the broad Col du Dard, 3153m.

From the col descend northwards on the Glacier de la Roche Ferran to the Refuge du Col de la Vanoise (Felix Faure Hut), 2516m. Be aware that this hut can be difficult to find in poor visibility.

For a few, with the smell of the fleshpots in their nostrils, the attraction of Pralognan, a hot shower and a fine meal may be too great. Certainly this traditional Vanoise village retains much charm and the descent is enjoyable, but not always at the end of a long day if the snow conditions are poor and your knees are weak! If that's the case, you'd bet-

Arrival at the Col des Chasseforêt

ter put on your hair shirt, wait until morning and save the pleasures of Pralognan for an early lunch.

Stage 4

The Grande Casse, 3852m, SW flank from the Refuge du Col de la Vanoise (Felix Faure Hut), 2516m

Ascent:	1339m
Descent:	2455m to Pralognan
Difficulty:	BSA. D. S4/5.
Principal Aspect:	SW
Time:	8–9 hours hut to hut

This magnificent mountain is the highpoint of the Savoie and a classic, albeit quite difficult ascent. There are no

Steep climbing on the ascent of the Grand Casse, 3852m

really easy routes to the summit for the ski mountaineer. The normal route from the Felix Faure is via the south-west face and has a 200m section of 45°, making this considerably more difficult than the rest of the tour. However, for skiers with the necessary ability it offers a logical addition to the tour and can be combined with a descent to the delights of Pralognan.

From the refuge descend towards the E bank of Lac Long and begin the steep ascent NE towards the northern tongue of the Glacier des Grands Couloirs (S3). The snout is steep and highly crevassed – climb it. Gradually the slope becomes less difficult, but remains relatively steep and crevassed. Continue climbing E to c.3350m, at which point a huge bergschrund (possible ski depot) is crossed and the slope above once again steepens (S4/S5) until the glacier flattens at c.3700m, before the Col des Grands Couloirs is reached. At this point climb directly and steeply up the south face of the Grande Casse to a point on the west ridge from where you can reach the summit. Descend by the same route.

Stage 4 or 5
Refuge du Col de la Vanoise (Felix Faure Hut), 2531m – Pralognan – Refuge de Péclet Polset, 2450m

Ascent:	1050m
Descent:	1131m
Difficulty:	SAM. A fine descent followed by a long, steady hut climb.
Principal Aspect:	W, S
Time:	6 hours

There is little advantage in leaving the hut too early. Descend directly to Pralognan for a second breakfast or an early lunch. There are plenty of good restaurants.

There are several descent options. Descend directly W either via the Lac des Assiettes and the Ruisseau de l'Arcelin to les Fontanettes or, alternatively, via Lac Long and the N side of the Lac des Vaches, and so reach the les Fontanettes via the Gliere valley.

The ascent to the Péclet Polset Refuge from Pralognan takes about 5 hours. If conditions allow it is possible to take a taxi part way and save a couple of hours of ascent. The hut is difficult to find in poor visibility.

However, returning to Aussois using local transport via Chambery and Modane is no easy matter either, and can take up to 8 hours.

From Pralognan follow the main valley of the Doron de Chaviere south along what in summer is the route of (GR55), one of the many variations of the GR5.

Stage 6
Refuge de Péclet Polset, 2450m – Dôme de Polset, 3326m – Refuge de Péclet Polset, 2450m

Ascent:	876m
Descent:	876m
Difficulty:	SAM. A relatively short day that can be combined with a descent to the valley.
Principal Aspect:	E, N
Time:	3 hours in ascent

This point can also be reached by ascending a narrow arm of the Glacier de Gebroulaz without climbing to the col, but this option depends on snow cover and the condition of the glacier. At c.2600m turn SE and negotiate the narrow glacier to pt.2943m.

From the hut set off in a NW direction to the glacier hollow that holds Lac Blanc, 2459m. Traverse around the N side of the lake and climb in a WNW direction as far as the Col du Soufre, 2819m. From the col descend SW to gain the Glacier de Gebroulaz at c.2750m. Continue climbing S to pt.2943m. ◀

From the vicinity of pt.2943m continue SSE, making a gradual ascent of the broad glacier, aiming to pass between two rock islands that extend N from the Dôme de Polset. Continue climbing more steeply to the summit of the Dôme de Polset, 3501m.

Either of the ascent routes can be followed in descent.

A fit party will be able to reach Modane or Aussois on the same day. The two options are described in Stage 7.

Stage 7
Refuge de Péclet Polset, 2450m, to Modane or Aussois

Ascent:	290m
Descent:	1500m to Modane
Difficulty:	SAM. Straightforward descent if the snow is good.
Principal Aspect:	N, S
Time:	3 hours

Via Modane – From the hut continue S following the route of the GR55 to reach the Col de Chaviere, 2796m. From the col descend to pt.2504, where the valley divides either side of the Tete Noir. The valley on the R goes via the Grand Planav, following the Ruisseau de St Bernard, to Polset and so to Modane. The other, going L, traverses the E flank of the Tete Noir more steeply and descends to the Refuge de l'Orgere above Modane.

Direct route to Aussois – this naturally completes the circle and crosses the Brèche de la Croix de la Rue, 2883m. Traverse SE from the refuge following a well-marked moraine valley in the direction of the Pointes de la Partie to reach pt.2488m. Continue below the moraine, climbing between it and the northern rim of the tiny Glacier Masse on the N flank of the Pointes de la Partie. Gain the crest of the moraine and continue climbing steeply E to reach the Brèche de la Croix de la Rue, 2883m. On the far side descend steeply into the valley of the Ruisseau de St Benoit, turning SE to reach the Refuge du Fond d'Aussois, 2324m. From the hut a short climb SE leads to the Refuge de la Dent Parrachée, 2511m.

From the hut descend SE to La Fournache and connect with the pistes leading to Aussois.

LA POULÉ: USEFUL INFORMATION

Huts
The huts are generally well equiped. There is also a central reservation system in operation.

Huts Central Reservation.
Tel: 04 79 08 71 49

Refuge Dent de la Parrachée, 2511m, CAF. Tel: 04 79 20 32 87/04 79 08 71 49 also 04 79 20 36 81. Feb to mid-May need to reserve. 30 places.

Refuge de l'Arpont 2309m (PNV). Tel: 04 79 20 51 51. 28 places in winter.

Refuge du Col de la Vanoise (Felix Faure Hut), 2517m.
Tel: 04 79 08 25 23/04 79 08 71 49 or 04 79 08 70 60. April and May – weekends on demand.

Refuge de Péclet Polset, 2450m. Tel: 04 79 08 72 13 or 04 79 08 71 57. 18 places in winter.

Refuge du Fond Aussois, 2210m. Tel: 04 79 20 39 83/ 04 79 05 96 70. 28

places in winter. Guarded 20 March–27 May.

Useful Contacts
Modane Office du Tourisme.
Tel: 04 79 05 28 58

Aussois Office de Tourisme.
Tel: 04 79 05 28 58

www.aussois.com
Pralongnan Office of Tourism.
Tel: 04 79 08 79 08
Fax: 04 79 08 76 74

Weather Information
Savoie. Tel: 08 36 68 02 73
Isère. Tel: 08 36 68 02 38

Emergency and Rescue
Police emergency. Tel: 112
Maurienne area CRS/PGHM.
Tel: 04 79 05 11 88
CRS Modane. Tel: 04 79 05 11 88
PGHM de Modane.
Tel: 04 79 05 50 98

GRAND PARADISO
HAUTE ROUTE

The Valdostaine Haute Route is a magnificent east to west traverse of the Grand Paradiso National Park. A quick look at the map will show you that the tour traverses the mountainous heart of the national park. This is a spectacular journey which crosses the grain of the country on a route that climbs in and out of the many deep valleys that dissect this wonderful region. But ups and downs are what ski touring is all about, and this strenuous tour provides them in both quantity and quality. Beginning in the Valnontey above Cogne, the route passes in turn through the Valsavaranche and Val di Rheimes before finally finishing in the ancient village of Valgrisenche by way of

Traversing below the Leveciau glacier and north-west face of the Grand Paradiso

some marvellous peaks, including the Grand Serra, Grand Paradiso, Cima di Entrelor, Becca della Traversière and Becca di Giasson.

The Grand Paradiso was established as a national park in 1922, the first in Italy to be recognised. Until then it had been the private hunting reserve of Italy's king, Vittorio Emanuele III, who gifted the area to the state. As a hunting reserve it had been well stocked for sport, so that today it benefits from abundant wildlife. It is not unusual during the spring to see ibex, chamois, marmot, squirrel, fox and rock partridge, as well as the less common ermine, ptarmigan, golden eagle, beaded vulture and raven. In addition to the diverse fauna, the deep valleys

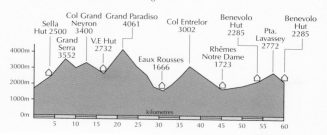

GRAND PARADISO HAUTE ROUTE Stages 1–5

GRAND PARADISO HAUTE ROUTE
Stages 6–7

are well forested, and the meadows and Alpine pastures display a wide range of Alpine flowers. The national park has worked to protect the ibex – and has suceeded so well that today ibex from the park are used to restock other Alpine areas where this spectacular creature has become all but extinct.

The area's highest summit, the Grand Paradiso, 4061m, is one of many spectacular peaks. The others, although lower, are no less impressive. In fact the area is a myriad of mountains, glaciers, permanent snowfields, bare rock and stunning lakes. The views from its peaks, ridges and cols are outstanding – one has a feeling of being surrounded by the sweeping arc of the Alps. The park retains a wonderfully isolated and wild feeling, enhanced by its rich flora and fauna. Despite the region's nearness to the cities of the Piedmont, the impact of man remains small – all the better for the lover of high mountains. As a mountainous national park the Grand Paradiso provides an enviable blueprint for other Alpine areas.

The many north–south valleys which dissect the park have been deepened by glacially fed rivers which eventually join the Dora Baltea flowing through the Val d'Aosta. These valleys provide the visitor with easy access right into the heart of the mountains.

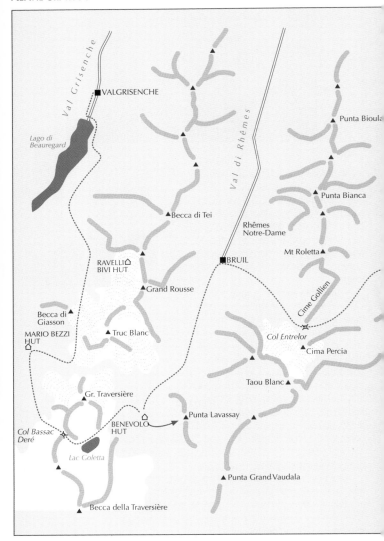

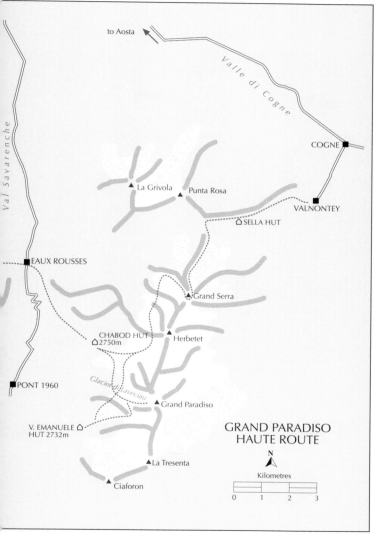

to Aosta

Valle di Cogne

COGNE

Val Savarenche

La Grivola

Punta Rosa

VALNONTEY

△ SELLA HUT

■ EAUX ROUSSES

▲ Grand Serra

CHABOD HUT
△ 2750m

Herbetet

■ PONT 1960

Glacier di Laveciau

▲ Grand Paradiso

V. EMANUELE △
HUT 2732m

GRAND PARADISO
HAUTE ROUTE

N

▲ La Tresenta

Kilometres

0   1   2   3

▲ Ciaforon

The Tour

Start:	Valnontey is the actual starting point, although Cogne in the Val d'Aosta provides a useful base.
Finish:	Valgrisenche
Duration:	7 days
Location:	Grand Paradiso National Park – Italy
Difficulty:	SAM. PD. A moderately strenuous tour with some long ascents and, at times, complex route-finding.
Best Time:	March–April
Facilities:	All shopping is best done in Aosta or in the main valley rather than in Cogne. All accommodation is in mountain huts.
Access:	Direct access to the Valnontey by road. Those travelling by their own transport may find it more convenient to park in Aosta and aim to reach Valnontey by public transport or taxi to begin the first stage.
Maps:	IGC 1:25,000 Grand Paradiso La Grivola Cogne. Kompass Sheet 86 1:50,000 Grand Paradiso Valle d'Aosta

ROUTE SUMMARY

Stage 1: Valnontey, 1696m, to the Rifugio Sella, 2584m
Stage 2: Rifugio Sella, 2584m – Grand Serra – Rifugio Vittorio Emanuele, 2732m
Stage 3: Vittoria Emanuele Hut – Grand Paradiso – Chabod Refuge – Eaux Rousses, 1666m
Stage 4: Eaux Rousses, 1666m – Rhêmes Notre-Dame, 1723m
Stage 5: Rhêmes Notre-Dame, 1723m – Benevolo Refuge, 2285m
Stage 6: Benevolo Refuge, 2285m – Becca della Traversière, 3337m – Rifugio Mario Bezzi, 2264m
Stage 7: Rifugio Mario Bezzi, 2264m – Becca di Giasson, 3202m – Valgrisenche

ROUTE ITINERARY
Stage 1
Valnontey, 1696m, to the Rifugio Sella, 2584m

Ascent:	888m
Difficulty:	Easy
Principal Aspect:	S
Time:	2 hours

After leaving the Val d'Aosta at Cogne for the valley of Valnontey, the first village you arrive at is Valnontey, a delightful place. From the car park next to the Giardino Alpina Paradisia, follow the main summer track through dense forest which leads into the Valle del Lauson. Invariably this section of the route will have to be climbed on foot until clear of the forest. Continue the ascent up the N bank of the Torrent Grand Lauson, staying below the cliffs of the Testa di Crocheneuille as far as the Rifugio Sella, 2584m. This is an easy and short day; one that can be combined with last-minute shopping or a long lunch!

Stage 2
Rifugio Sella, 2584m – Grand Serra – Rifugio Vittorio Emanuele, 2732m

Ascent:	1600m
Descent:	1545m
Difficulty:	Long and strenuous day with several escape possiblities.
Principal Aspect:	N in ascent. W mainly in descent.
Time:	8–10 hours

In sharp contrast with Stage 1, this is a demanding day with complicated route-finding and is best undertaken in good visibility and stable conditions. The ascent of the Grand Serra, 3552m, should not be underestimated and represents only a part of the day's route. Although this is a complex and relatively long day there are at least two escape possibilities to the Val Savaranche should the need arise.

From the hut begin by skinning easily W as far as an obvious rock, which forms a natural reservoir, before

First climb of the day

Escape To Eaux Rousses

Should conditions demand a change of plan or an escape route, it is possible to descend directly to Eaux Rousses in the Val Savarenche. However, making the descent would bypass the key section of this delightful expedition. If circumstances change it is possible to go by road from Eaux Rousses to Alp Pravieux and climb to the Chabod Refuge, from where an enjoyable ascent/descent of Grand Paradiso can be still be made.

turning SW in a wide hollow towards the distinctive Torrione Giallo. Continue the ascent over undulating moraine-covered slopes to reach the snout of the Lauson Glacier at c.2900m. Ascend the glacier more steeply, bearing SE to reach a shoulder at c.3300m. At this point cross to the Glacier Grand Val, climbing diagonally S to reach the east ridge of the Grand Serra close to pt.3475m. Continue on foot up the straightforward rocks of the east ridge to the summit.

On a fine day the summit of the Grand Serra provides a magnificent balcony from which to view the surrounding mountains, notably the Grivola, 3969m, to the north and the Grand Paradiso, 4061m, to the south. More than anything, however, it is the wild setting of this corner of the Eastern Graians that is most impressive and undoubtedly lends a special charm to this alternative Valdostaine Haute Route.

From the summit descend the north ridge on foot to reach the skiing on the more amenable Timorion Glacier. Descend the glacier, more or less in a westerly direction, to reach the boundary of its true left bank below pt.3107m. ◀

From below pt.3107m, instead of descending to the Val Savarenche continue S by traversing moraine slopes and a mulde to reach the true right bank of the Glacier di Grand Neyron. Continue SW, skirting the the toe of the north-west ridge of the Herbetet at c.3000m before climbing more steeply southwards to reach the Col Grand Neyron, 3414m. On the S side of the col you will find the conveniently placed Sberna Bivouac hut, which has room for six. From the col climb a short way E along the ridge towards the Herbetet before attempting to gain the Montandayne Glacier.

Make a gently descending traverse SSW on the Montandayne Glacier, passing beneath rock buttresses and glacier bays as you traverse below the impressive north-west face of Grand Paradiso. All the while aim for pt.3089m at the base of a rock buttress marking the true left bank of the crevassed Laveciau Glacier (be aware that these run parallel with your route of descent) and continue as far as a distinctive lateral moraine. Now make a traverse, more or less along the 3000m contour, skirting a rock buttress until the VE Refuge comes into view. Descend towards it, crossing moraine-covered slopes before joining the well-marked 'normal route' to and from the Grand Paradiso to arrive at the distinctive Vittorio Emanuele Refuge, 2732m. ▶

Descent to the Rifugio Chabod and Val Savaranche

If you wish to cut short the traverse to the Vittorio Emanuele, it is possible to descend directly to the comfortable Rifugio Chabod and the Val Savaranche when you gain the Montandayne Glacier. To do this descend the glacier SW towards pt.3032m. Once off the glacier descend slopes N of the Costa Savolere torrent to the well-positioned Chabod Refuge. From the refuge it is possible to descend directly to the road at Alp Pravieux, 1834m, in the Val Savarenche and so avoid the traverse to the Vittoria Emanuele Refuge. Alternatively you can stay at the hut and ascend the Grand Paradiso from there.

Surrounding the Madonna on the Grand Paradiso

Ascent of the Grand Paradiso from Chabod Refuge, 2750m

Ascent:	1311m
Descent:	1311m to the Chabod Hut
Difficulty:	PD. A long climb with several steep sections and a short final scramble to reach the summit Madonna.
Principal Aspect:	N and N
Time:	4–6 hours in ascent

If for some reason you cut short the traverse to the Vittoria Emanuele Hut and descend to the Chabod Refuge it is still possible to make an ascent of Grand Paradiso from there and descend to the Val Savaranche, and thus remain on course.

From the hut climb back to the Montandayne Glacier at *c*.3032m before making a diagonal ascent SE towards pt.3252m below the impressive north-west face of Grand Paradiso. Make an ascending traverse of the Laveciau Glacier towards pt.3432m below the Sciena d'Asino, finding the easiest line through crevasses to reach the broad glacier shoulder that forms the north-west ridge of the Becca di Montcorve, 3875m. At this point the normal route from the Rifugio Vittorio Emanuele is joined. Follow the broad slopes of the north-west ridge in a broad sweep SE until it is possible to traverse diagonally L, beneath the impressive pinnacle of Il Roc, 4026m, towards the jagged rocky crest that is the summit ridge of the Grand Paradiso. It is normal to leave skis in the vicinity of the bergschrund before making a final scramble to the Madonna, perched on a rocky tower a short way from the true summit. This awkward scramble can be easily rope protected.

From the ski depot descend the route of ascent towards the Schiena d'Asino and descend by the route of ascent to the Chabod Refuge.

Stage 3
Vittoria Emanuele Hut – Grand Paradiso – Chabod Refuge – Eaux Rousses

Ascent:	1329m
Descent:	2373m
Difficulty:	F. A long easy climb with a short rocky scramble to reach the Madonna. Magnificent views. A long and beautiful descent.
Principal Aspect:	W and S in ascent. N in descent.
Time:	4–6 hours in ascent

The ascent of the Grand Paradiso is the highpoint of this tour – and not simply because the mountain is a 4000er and the highest summit in the Graians, although that in itself is pretty significant for mountaineers. The mountain was first climbed in 1860 by British alpinists J. Cowell and W. Dundas with two celebrated Chamonix guides, Michel Payot and Jean Tairraz, after a prodigious bout of step-cutting and an arrested fall. The mountain was not skied until those great pioneers of ski mountaineering and hard rock climbing, Paul Preuss and W. von Bergnuth, reached the summit in the winter of 1913.

From the hut climb diagonally NE into the broad mulde of the Grand Paradiso Glacier. Ascend the glacier, via two steeper sections; the first is taken on the left, the second on the right until gentler slopes then lead to a narrowing. The route continues along the glacier's edge to a saddle below the Becco del Moncorve at about 3800m, which rises above the drop of the mountain's steep south face. Now ascend diagonally N (possible crevasses) across steeper slopes below the impressive pinnacle of Il Roc, 4026m, before continuing towards the jagged rocky crest that is the summit ridge of the Grand Paradiso. After crossing the bergschrund it is normal to leave skis before making the final scramble (bolt protected) to the Madonna, which is perched on a rocky tower, about 15 minutes' scrambling from the true summit at the NW end of the ridge. Most skiers seem to stop at the Madonna.

From the summit return to your skis and begin the descent. Initially follow your route of ascent as far as the saddle below the Becco del Moncorve. Then descend NW along the well-defined edge of the Grand Paradiso towards the Schiena d'Asino. After that bear N at c.3500m onto the Laveciau Glacier through an area of crevasses before bearing N on a descending traverse towards pt.3252m. Continue the diagonal descent below the Point Farrar and Point Vaccarone towards the edge of the Montandayne Glacier at pt.3032m. From the edge of the glacier descend moraine slopes directly to the Chabod Refuge.

If you have booked accommodation in Eaux Rousses or Degioz it is possible to continue directly to Alp Pravieux in the Val Savaranche, a further 900m of descent. The descent is invariably interesting through meadows and forest. Customarily you have to carry your skis once low down in the forest, especially later in the season, but the descent is an altogether long and enjoyable one. It is not unusual to see chamois and ibex on this part of the tour.

Stage 4
Eaux Rousses, 1666m – Rhêmes Notre-Dame, 1723m

Ascent:	1356m
Descent:	1279m
Difficulty:	F. In the right conditions this stage can provide much delightful skiing.
Principal Aspect:	East in ascent. W in descent.
Time:	6 hours

The route from Eaux Rousses follows a good path, the Alta Via della Valle d'Aosta, which zigzags NW through the woods to a former royal hunting lodge, the Cas Orvielle (2164m). From here there are two options: either continue along the summer path, or if the snow cover is good go southwards to gain the Nampio valley – where once again it is not unusual to see ibex and chamois. Continue SW through the valley, skirting the Lago Djuan and Lago Nero before climbing more steeply to reach the Colle di Entrelor, 3002m. If the conditions are suitable it is possible to gain the summit of the Cima di Percia Nord by heading S from the col.

From the col aim westwards for the Vallon di Entrelon by skiing a series of enjoyable pitches to an alp at c.2140m. Given good snow cover the next stage of the descent can be most enjoyable. Continue through tall forest, going N along the sumer track until you reach the peaceful ski resort of Rhêmes Notre-Dame, 1723m. It has a resident population of around 90 inhabitants,

Climbing through widely spaced pine trees is typical of terrain encountered in the valleys on the Grand Paradiso Haute Route

and sports seven hotels and a restaurant. With a variety of lifts and some good off-piste skiing it is a first-rate place for a lay-over day if one is needed. ▶

Stage 5
Rhêmes Notre-Dame, 1723 – Benevolo Refuge, 2285m

Ascent:	562m to the refuge
Difficulty:	An easy hut day – often combined with a peak close to the hut.
Principal Aspect:	N and E
Time:	2 hours

Alternative Route from Eaux Rousse to Rhêmes Notre-Dame

Follow the route described above into the Nampio valley towards Lake Djuan. Skirt around the lake to the E and continue heading S, climbing gently to cross the ridge of the Costa la Manteau. Make a diagonal descent into the Valle d'Meyes before turning W following the valley to the Percia Glacier. Ascend its gentle slopes SW towards the Cima di Entrelor, 3430m. The glacier col can be crossed north of the peak, which can be climbed easily. Descend the tiny Entrelor Glacier on the W side of the ridge and continue NW into the Entrelor valley, which is followed to the alp at 2142m. Continue the descent to Bruil and the tiny picturesque village of Rhêmes Notre-Dame.

This is a poular hut for ski tourers and is easily reached from Rhêmes Notre-Dame. If the hut is your only objective it must surely be considered a rest day.

If you arrive at the hut early there is plenty that can be combined with the climb. You can continue beyond the hut, skinning E, and make an ascent of around 500m to the fine summit of the Punta di Lavassay, 2772m. In the right snow conditions it offers agreeable skiing back to the hut and enough exercise to prepare you for the evening meal.

From Rhêmes it is possible to continue directly up the road to Thumel, 1868m, snow conditions permitting. From there continue up the west side of the valley, crossing rather steep slopes and frequently the remains of avalanches to reach a bridge. Cross the bridge and continue along the summer path to the hospitable Benevolo Hut.

The Benevolo provides a wonderful base from which to bag several perfect ski summits. Both the hospitality and food at the hut are outstanding, so much so that it is sometimes hard to leave and finish the tour!

The Benevolo Hut is also also a good staging post for tourers traversing between the Grand Paradiso and

Ski depot close to the bergscrund below the Grand Paradiso, with the distinctive pinnacle of Il Roc, 4026m, beyond

Vanoise regions. Because of this it can be a busy place, so it is important to book your place well in advance and confirm your arrival.

Stage 6
Benevolo Refuge, 2285m – Becca della Traversière, 3337m – Rifugio Mario Bezzi, 2264m

Ascent:	1052m
Descent:	1073m
Difficulty:	F. A demanding day that requires good visibility and stable snow conditions.
Principal Aspect:	N and E in ascent. N and W in descent.
Time:	6–8 hours

From the hut go S towards the Truc St Elana keeping below rock outcrops to the R. After a few minutes climb W, finding a way up through steep terrain to a ridge bordering the Goletta glacier, which fills the upper basin of the Comba di Goletta. Continue SW, gaining the glacier, and climb towards the summit of the Becca della Traversière, 3337m. Gain its east ridge close to the summit and follow this to the top. If conditions for the summit climb are not good it is possible to avoid the climb by traversing south of the glacial lake di Goletta to cross the Col Bassac Deré, 3082m, which is the low point on the north ridge of the Becca della Traversière. Cross this to gain the Glacier di Gliairetta.

If the summit of the Becca della Traversière can be climbed, then it is possible to descend its north ridge a short way towards pt.3196m and so gain the slopes of the Glacier di Gliairetta. From the col and summit there are splendid views of the Aiguille de la Sassière, 3751m, itself a magnificent ski peak, but one that is normally done from the French (W) flank.

Both routes now follow the same course. Descend the glacier NW which is quite straightforward. At c.2900m the glacier narrows and and falls N, at which point it becomes the Glacier di Vaudet. It is essential to

97

keep to the true right (E) bank to avoid crevasses. Continue descending northwards down the now flat valley floor to the Mario Bezzi Refuge, 2264m. This hut is not always guarded, therefore it is essential to find out if the guardian is present or else carry provisions for your stay in the winter room.

Stage 7
Rifugio Mario Bezzi, 2264m – Becca di Giasson, 3202m – Valgrisenche

Ascent:	938m
Descent:	1538m
Difficulty:	F. An easy peak followed by a wonderful descent
Principal Aspect:	W and N
Time:	6 hours

From the hut return S in the valley a short way until it is possible to turn L (E) and climb steeply to gain the meadows of the Piano di Vaudet and cross a repetitive series of hollows and ridges. At c.2800m turn NE to skirt the edge of the small San Martino Glacier at pt.2883m and reach the tiny Col di Giasson, 3154m. From the col the somewhat inconspicuous summit of the Becca di Giasson is reached without problems by a 100m climb to the W.

From the summit ski N down the slopes of the Glacier di Giasson and follow the valley NW towards the Lago di Beauregard – retained by a huge dam with an in-situ climbing wall. Eventually an open larch forest is reached. It is possible to descend directly to the road skirting the reservoir, which you then plod around to the well-preserved medieval town of Valgrisenche. Alternatively, make a descending traverse NNE along the margin of the forest until a fire break, above the hamlet of La Rotse, allows a descent to the road. This is then followed to the delightful resort of Valgrisenche and a welcome celebration at the end of a splendid haute route.

*Making the most of
some fresh powder by
putting in first tracks*

GRAND PARADISO HAUTE ROUTE: USEFUL INFORMATION

Huts
Benevolo Hut.
Tel: 0165 936143/0165 765696
Vittoria Emanuele Hut (new).
Tel: 0165 95920/0165 95103
Federico Chabod Hut.
Tel: 0165 95574/0165 905798
Vittorio Sella Hut.
Tel: +39 0165 74310

Useful Contacts
Tourist information. Valgrisenche
Tel. +39 165 9719
Weather information.
Tel: 1678 37077
Police emergency. Tel: 113

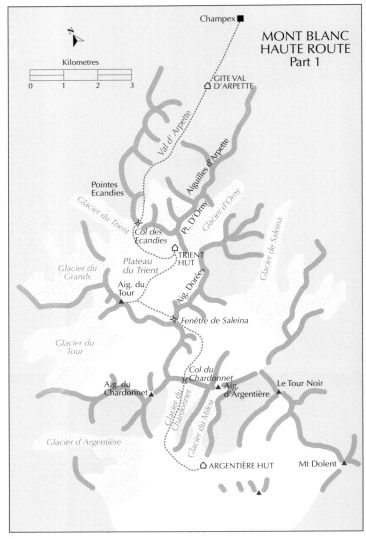

Champex

MONT BLANC
HAUTE ROUTE
Part 1

N

Kilometres

0   1   2   3

GITE VAL
D'ARPETTE

Val d' Arpette

Aiguilles d'Arpette

Pointes
Ecandies

Glacier du Trient

Pt. D'Orny

Glacier d'Orny

Glacier de Saleina

Col des
Ecandies

TRIENT
HUT

Plateau
du Trient

Glacier du
Grands

Aig. du
Tour

Aig. Dorées

Fenêtre de Saleina

Glacier du
Tour

Col du
Chardonnet

Aig. du
Chardonnet

Glacier du Chardonnet

Aig.
d'Argentière

Le Tour Noir

Glacier du Milieu

Glacier d'Argentière

ARGENTIÈRE HUT

Mt Dolent

MONT BLANC HAUTE ROUTE

No hut-to-hut traverse across the magnificent mountains and glaciers of the Mont Blanc range is likely to be straightforward. The mountains are high, the glaciers complicated and the days necessarily long. The rewards, however, are commensurate with the effort, and any ski mountaineer who completes this demanding and serious high-level *tour de force* will take away a lasting memory and a well-deserved glow of satisfaction.

Several big traverses have been made across the Mont Blanc massif. Some of them, not so long ago, would have been classified as 'ski extreme'. Most were integrals connecting a series of summer grand courses, following airy snow arêtes, and involved difficult mixed climbing and descents of very steep couloirs and faces – by and large they were not ideal as ski routes, but skis made them possible at the time. They were largely one-offs, defining the possible by undertaking the seemingly imposssible. That's just the kind of alpinism that around Chamonix is commonplace.

This tour, on the other hand, although a difficult and serious one, is within the compass of competent and acclimatised ski mountaineers. What's more, it is a logical ski route, where skiing is the preferred option and the need to carry skis is infrequent but essential.

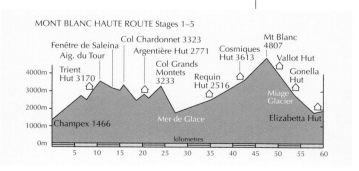

MONT BLANC HAUTE ROUTE Stages 1–5

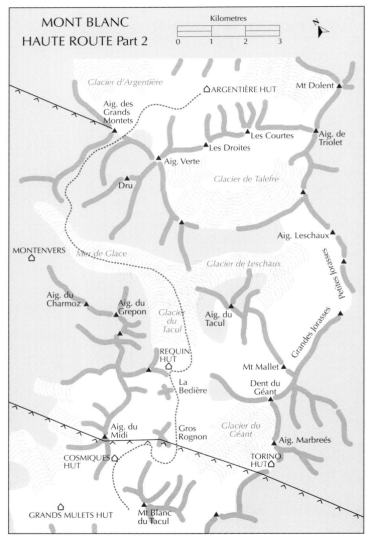

MONT BLANC
HAUTE ROUTE Part 2

Kilometres

0   1   2   3

N

Glacier d'Argentière

△ ARGENTIÈRE HUT

Mt Dolent ▲

Aig. des
Grands
Montets ▲

Les Courtes ▲

Aig. de
Triolet ▲

Les Droites ▲

Aig. Verte ▲

Glacier de Talefre

Dru ▲

Aig. Leschaux ▲

MONTENVERS
△

Mer de Glace

Glacier de Leschaux

Petites Jorasses

Aig. du
Charmoz ▲

Aig. du
Grepon ▲

*Glacier
du
Tacul*

Aig. du
Tacul ▲

Grandes Jorasses

REQUIN
HUT
△

Mt Mallet ▲

La
Bedière

Dent du
Géant ▲

Aig. du
Midi ▲

Gros
Rognon

*Glacier du
Géant*

Aig. Marbreés ▲

COSMIQUES △
HUT

TORINO
HUT △

△
GRANDS MULETS HUT

Mt Blanc
du Tacul ▲

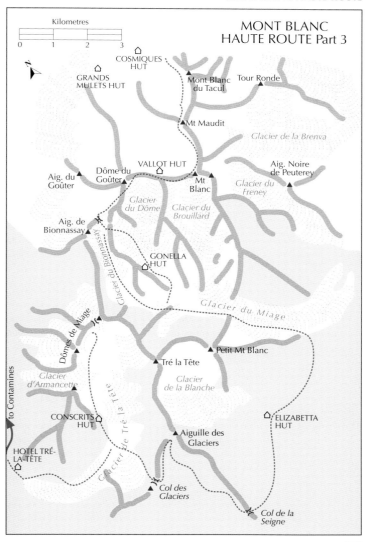

Kilometres
0   1   2   3

N

MONT BLANC
HAUTE ROUTE Part 3

COSMIQUES
HUT

GRANDS
MULETS HUT

Mont Blanc
du Tacul

Tour Ronde

Mt Maudit

Glacier de la Brenva

VALLOT HUT

Aig. du
Goûter

Dôme du
Goûter

Mt
Blanc

Aig. Noire
de Peuterey

*Glacier du
Freney*

*Glacier
du Dôme*

*Glacier du
Brouillard*

Aig. de
Bionnassay

Glacier du Bionnassay

GONELLA
HUT

Glacier du Miage

Dômes de Miage

Petit Mt Blanc

Tré la Tête

*Glacier
de la Blanche*

*Glacier
d'Armancette*

Glacier de Tré la Tête

to Contamines

CONSCRITS
HUT

ELIZABETTA
HUT

Aiguille des
Glaciers

HOTEL TRÉ-
LA-TÊTE

*Col des
Glaciers*

*Col de la
Seigne*

103

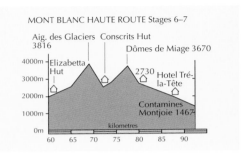

MONT BLANC HAUTE ROUTE Stages 6–7

The main challenge of the tour is the traverse of Mont Blanc. It is avoidable, but if the route is to have any meaning as the Mont Blanc Haute Route the traverse over the summit must surely be made. The alternatives, although still enjoyable, are really second best. You can take either the bus from Chamonix to Contamines, followed by an ascent to the Conscrits Hut or, preferably, a descent of the Glacier de Toule to Entrèves followed by a slog or taxi into the Val Veni to regain the route at the Elizabetta Refuge. But without Mont Blanc the Mont Blanc Haute Route is incomplete.

It goes without saying that a high level of fitness and acclimatisation will be important factors on this tour, along with solid skills in all aspects of mountaineering – not the least judgement and route-finding. In addition, good weather and conditions are essential. This is not the kind of tour where you fall readily into the tracks of endless parties following a well-worn path. However, it does cross other well-known routes, in particular the High Level Route and the popular Vallée Blanche descent – both against the flow of whatever traffic is on them. On the other hand, as the journey progresses it leaves the well known for the untracked and infrequently travelled corners of the range, and during its course the route frequently crosses between Switzerland, France and Italy.

The route described is the purest line. If time is a key factor then instead of climbing to the Requin Hut after descending to the Mer de Glace, it is possible to descend

A 'donkey' over the dome of Mont Blanc: distinctive lenticular clouds herald bad weather and a change of plans

to Chamonix and use the Aigiuille du Midi cable car to reach the Cosmiques Hut on the same day, given that the lift is running.

The Tour

Start:	Champex
Finish:	les Contamines Montjoie
Duration:	7 perfect days
Location:	The Mont Blanc range and the route of this tour straddles three countries, Switzerland, France and Italy. The route begins in Champex, close to Martigny in the Swiss Valais, crosses the border into Haute Savoie in France and makes a brief visit to Italy before returning to Haute Savoie.
Difficulty:	BSA. AD+. A high-level traverse through serious glacial terrain which includes ascents of high mountains and passes, including the traverse of Mont Blanc. TBSA – D if the most difficult options are taken.
Best Time:	April–June. Ski lifts close early May. Longer days later in the season are useful but the final descent becomes more difficult. Crevasses are more evident later in the season, especially on the south side of Mont Blanc.
Facilities:	There are plenty of hotels and pensions in Champex. Food and last minute equipment buys are also possible in the

village. If the Val d'Arpette is short of snow a taxi can be taken as far as the Relais d'Arpette and saves walking up the road. If open, the Relais d'Arpette is a good place to stay.

Access:

Geneva is the nearest airport from where Champex can be reached directly and easily by a combination of rail and post-bus. At the end of the tour there is bus from Contamines Montjoie to the railway station at St Gervais, and from there a train to Geneva. The whole area is well served by road, rail and bus connections.

Maps:

Two IGN maps cover the complete Mont Blanc range. They are IGN Chamonix Massif du Mt Blanc 3630 OT, IGN St Gervais 3531 ET.

ROUTE SUMMARY

Stage 1: Champex, 1466m – Val d'Arpette – Trient Hut, 3170m

Stage 2: Trient Hut, 3170m – Aiguille du Tour, 3542m – Fenêtre de Saleina – Col du Chardonnet, 3323m – Argentière Hut, 2771m

Ascending Mont Blanc above the Grands Mulets Hut

Stage 3: Argentière Hut, 2771m – Col des Grands Montets, 3233m – Pas de Chèvre – Requin Hut, 3516m

Stage 4: Requin Hut, 2516m – Cosmiques Hut, 3613m
Stage 5: Cosmiques Hut, 3613m – Mont Blanc Traverse, 4807m – Gonella Hut, 3071m
Stage 6: Gonella Hut, 3071m – Col de la Seigne, 2516m – Aiguille des Glaciers, 3816m – Conscrits Hut, 2730m
Stage 7: Conscrits Hut, 2730m – Dômes de Miage, 3670m – les Contamines Montjoie, 1467m

ROUTE ITINERARY
Stage 1
Champex, 1466m – Val d'Arpette – Col des Ecandies, 2796m or Fenêtre du Chamois – Trient Hut, 3170m

Ascent:	1704m
Descent:	50m
Difficulty:	A tiring first day involving a long climb. Avalanche danger exists in the Val d'Arpette, especially later in the day, so an early start is advised. Steep cramponing in the Couloir des Chamois or crevasses to negotiate alongside the Trient glacier's icefall.
Principal Aspect:	E, NW
Time:	5–6 hours

The delightfully situated Swiss village of Champex is the starting point of this traverse. It will be familiar to anyone who has completed the High Level Route between Chamonix and Zermatt.

From Champex follow the long Val d'Arpette to its end, climbing into the Combe des Ecandies. There is a choice of routes to reach the Trient Plateau. Either cross the Col des Ecandies and traverse to the SW around the foot of the rocks of the Petite Pointe d'Orny. Then ascend the small steep icefall, crossing several crevasses, but staying close to the rocks to reach easier ground above. Alternatively, the same point on the Trient Plateau can be reached by climbing the steep snow Couloir des Chamois, left of the Col des Ecandies, to the Fenêtre du Chamois. In good conditions this is the quickest option.

Continue SE, climbing gently to the well-positioned Trient hut.

Stage 2

Trient Hut, 3170m – Aiguille du Tour, 3542m – Fenêtre de Saleina – Col du Chardonnet, 3323m – Argentière Hut, 2771m

Ascent:	892mm
Descent:	1333m
Difficulty:	BSA. Steep descent of Col de Saleina. Steep ascent of Col du Chardonnet. Highly crevassed glacier terrain.
Principal Aspect:	E, W
Time:	5–6 hours

The Aiguille du Tour is an enjoyable option. Cross the Plateau du Trient in a broad arc first to the SW and then the W, climbing towards the Aiguille du Tour. The S summit pt.3542m is the one to climb. If well snowed up, make a ski depot as high as possible before climbing the couloir to a notch between the two summits. At the ridge turn L and follow it past several small rock pinnacles to the summit. Descend by the same route.

From the ski depot, descend easily towards the Col du Tour, 3289m, before traversing to the Col de Saleina. Descend steeply to the Glacier de Saleina before traversing SW around the toe of the Grand Fourche. Continue SW, in full view of the magnificent north face of the Aiguille d'Argentière towards the Col du Chardonnet. After a short climb gain the base of the Col du Chardonnet. Carrying skis, cross the bergschrund and climb the steep couloir for 100m to the magnificent Col du Chardonnet. The views from here, across the basin of the Argentière of the huge wall of rock and ice which includes the Verte and Droites, has few equals in the Alps. What's more, the panorama improves during the descent as the Argentière basin opens out to reveal the equally impressive Courtes, Triolet and Dolent.

On the far side of the col descend the Glacier du Chardonnet more or less in the centre as far as c.3500m. Bear left and find the easiest line down the

true left bank to reach the Glacier d'Argentière. Turn L and climb easily up the glacier, staying on its true right bank until its lateral moraine is followed to the Argentière Refuge, 2771m.

The Dru and Mont Blanc seen from the start of the descent of the Pas des Chèvres from the Col Grands Montets

Stage 3

Argentière Hut 2771m – Col des Grands Montets 3233m – Pas de Chèvre – Requin Hut 2516m

Ascent:	1276m
Descent:	1433m
Difficulty:	BSA. The descent of the Pas des Chèvre is steep in the upper couloir. The lower section through the morain leading to the Mer de Glace may well be free of skiable snow later in the season and may have to be descended on foot.
Principal Aspect:	E in ascent. W in descent.
Time:	6–8 hours

From the hut regain the glacier and descend NW towards the base of the rognon below the Aiguille des Grands Montets. Now climb steeply W to reach the Col des Grands Montets. This reverses a popular off-piste descent route and is likely to be well tracked when the Grands Montets lift is working! If the lifts are running, and you don't feel like skiing against the flow, consider descending to the Lognan station and taking the cable car to the Grands Montets. This is not an option during May, when the lifts are closed.

Steeper and deeper just about sums up ski mountaineering around Mont Blanc – at the top of the Gervasutti Couloir on the Tour Ronde, with Mont Maudit beyond

From the Col des Grands Montets descend the Glacier des Grands Montets to the W, initially over broad gentle slopes, towards the Pas des Chèvre. In the early morning this slope is likely to be icy in places – it is certainly a better slope to ski after midday. As the slope steepens bear R into a broad open couloir. Ahead the slope is divided by a rock ridge with a snow couloir on either side.

Descend the right-hand couloir, which is steep and narrow in places, but usually well tracked if the lifts are running and the conditions favourable. From c.2600m the gully opens out and the skiing becomes more reasonable. Follow delightful slopes, below the impressive monolith of the Dru, bearing diagonally left to 2100m. Cross the moraine to the left and make a diagonal descent S, aiming for a lone tree on an escarpment between the Bayer and Chausettes streams. Descend through bushes and trees below cliffs and frozen waterfalls to reach a well-marked gully in the moraine that provides access to the Mer de Glace. It is important to find this gully, which is often unskiable (in which case descend to the glacier on foot). There is a second, less used gully higher up the moraine that also provides accesss to the glacier.

At this point you have two options: either descend to Chamonix and take the cable car to the Aiguille du Midi and spend the night in the Cosmiques Hut or contine up the Mer de Glace to the Requin Hut. Both are logical routes, although the former may not appeal to the purist. On the plus side it saves a day.

To reach the Requin Hut cross the glacier diagonally towards its true left bank and begin the long, slow ascent, more or less up its centre, without difficulty. In the season huge numbers of skiers will be descending the Mer de Glace, having skied the Vallée Blanche from the Aiguille du Midi. Keep climbing, following the glacier as it bends around the base of the Chamonix Aiguilles as far a flat expanse of ice below the impressive Géant icefall known as the Salle à Manger. The hut is on a rocky platform to the R and can be reached by a short, steep climb to a point left of the hut where a horizontal traverse leads to its marvellously positioned terrace.

Stage 4
Requin Hut, 2516m – Cosmiques Hut, 3613m

Ascent:	1100m
Difficulty:	A highly crevassed glacier ascent, especially later in the season when the crevasses are more open and the piste from the Aiguille du Midi is no longer evident.
Principal Aspect:	E
Time:	3–4 hours

From the Requin Hut reverse the popular La Bedière descent of the Vallée Blanche around the S side of the Gros Rognon as far as the Col du Midi. A short day, not exactly a rest day, but one that will allow a fresh start before the key ascent of Mont Blanc.

Leave the Requin Hut and traverse more or less horizontally SW towards the base of the Petite Rognon. In recent years there has been a reasonable way through the Seracs du Géant, keeping well to the right as you look up the icefall. This follows a series of easy steps which lead to a plateau above the icefall called La Bedière. Now continue S across a wide expanse of glacier climbing to *c*.3000m before making a broad arc to the W towards the Pyramide du Tacul. Then turn N to gain the Col du Gros Rognon, 3415m.

From the col bear W climbing around the base of the rocky northern facet of Mont Blanc du Tacul to reach the shadowy slope of the Mont Blanc du Tacul's north face at *c*.3600m. Its left-hand margin is defined by the rocks and couloirs of the Triangle du Mont Blanc du Tacul. The Cosmiques Hut is perched on a rocky knoll close by.

The Cosmiques Hut with the north-west face of Mont Blanc du Tacul beyond – the hut offers the best starting point for a traverse of Mont Blanc

Stage 5
Cosmiques Hut, 3613m – Mont Blanc Traverse, 4807m – Gonella Hut, 3071m

By whatever route it is done the traverse of Mont Blanc is a major undertaking at altitude. It is worth remember-

Ascent:	1250m
Descent:	1736m to the Gonella Hut
Difficulty:	PD+. AD. The key to the whole tour and a major undertaking. Steep climbing, sometimes on foot, combined with high altitude and serious glacier terrain.
Principal Aspect:	NW, N, NE
Time:	10–12 hours

ing that the first ski ascent of Mont Blanc was made in 1904 by Mylius, Tannler, Maurer and Zurfluh in February! The first traverse on skis was completed by von Tscharner and Wieland in April 1924.

The north face of Mont Blanc du Tacul is in fact a steep glacier, with seracs, crevasses and sometimes a wide bergschrund. Gain the foot of this slope on its left-hand side below a barrier of seracs and quickly make a diagonal traverse R into the centre of the slope. Continue the ascent in a series of steep steps, sometimes around impressive crevasses, going close to a number of seracs which vary in shape and size from year to year and can present considerable danger. It is often necessary to remove skis and climb steeper sections and small ice walls. The exact route varies from season to season, but the general line, if no track is in place, aims to gain the shoulder of the mountain's west ridge at c.4000m.

From the shoulder make a diagonal descent to the Col Maudit, from where a slanting ascent across the N face of Mont Maudit leads to the foot of the steep slope leading to the Col du Mont Maudit, 4345m. This slope has a number of steep steps, is exposed and can be icy. The final steep 100m is best climbed carrying skis.

From the col continue traversing the steep exposed slopes on the west flank of Mont Maudit to reach the Col de la Brenva, 4303m. Once it is safe to do so return to skis and continue the ascent southwards. The Mur de la Cote is also steep and may best be climbed on foot, after which more reasonable slopes lead to the summit.

From the summit descend the Bosses Arête, on foot, to the Vallot Hut, 4362m. ▶

Note: The Vallot Hut is for emergency use only and should not be used as a planned stop-over point. It is usually fairly squalid inside: it has an emergency phone and blankets but no stove.

At this point you have an important decision to make about snow conditions for the descent to the Gonella Hut. If you feel it is too late or conditions are poor it is best to spend the night at the Goûter Hut. If weather conditions are changing, the fastest descent to the valley is via the Grands Mulets.

Gonella Hut: To reach the Gonella Hut from the Vallot descend NW towards the Dôme du Goûter, skirting it to the S, before bearing SW on the French side of the ridge dividing France and Italy. The ridge narrows dramatically and should be descended on foot to the Col du Bionnassay, 3888m. From the col descend steeply to the S, into Italy, to gain the crest of the Col des Aiguille Grises, 3810m. Turn a rock outcrop on the right and descend steeply to the upper basin of the west branch of the Glacier du Dôme. Descend the glacier, which is highly crevassed, more or less in the centre, until at *c.*3400m bear R to find the easiest line down the west bank of the glacier. Leave the glacier a little above pt.3027m to reach the hut located on a rocky spur of the Aiguille Grises.

Looking towards the Bosses Arête and the summit of Mont Blanc from near the Vallot Hut

Descent Via the Bionnassay Glacier: In good snow conditions the most direct descent to the valley can be made via the Bionnassay Glacier on the Italian side. This is a steep, narrow and highly crevassed glacier, which merges with the Miage Glacier low down. In good snow conditions this gives the fastest route of descent, bypassing the Gonella Hut and instead descending directly to the Val Veni and the Elisabetta Hut.

Stage 6

Gonella Hut, 3071m – Col de la Seigne, 2516m – Aiguille des Glaciers, 3816m – Conscrits Hut, 2730m

Ascent:	1858m
Descent:	2199m
Difficulty:	AD. A major day in both time and effort which can be broken at the Elizabetta Hut or (with a deviation) at the private Robert Blanc Hut at the head of the Combe Noir on the south side of the Aiguille des Glaciers.
Principal Aspect:	SW, NW
Time:	10–12 hours

The possibility of another full day in paradise. The ascent of the Aiguille des Glaciers is a fine one and was first achieved on skis by two outstanding guides, Armand Charlet and Camille Devouassoux, on 24 May 1925.

In good snow conditions it is possible to descend the highly crevassed Glacier du Dôme directly to the gentle Miage Glacier. Alternatively, in slight snow cover a descent to the Miage Glacier via the summer track can be made, which is delicate and is best done on foot.

From the hut cross a rocky spur to the SW and then traverse a snowfield bearing S to make a diagonal descent of the E side of the rocky spur of the Aiguille Grises to a shoulder. Turn the shoulder and descend snow slopes to the Glacier du Miage. Descend this, keeping to the right bank, to reach the moraines above Lac du Combal and descend to the flat valley floor.

Difficult snow conditions on Mont Maudit during a traverse of Mont Blanc

Turn W and climb gently to the Elizabetta Refuge. Continue past the refuge and climb more steeply towards the Col de la Seigne, 2516m, the frontier between Italy and France. Someway before the col it may be possible to bear R and gain the frontier ridge N of the col at pt.2747m. From the ridge bear NW and climb steeply to a snow saddle on the south-west ridge (les Cabottes) of the Petite Aiguille des Glaciers, between pt.3000m and pt.3102m. If the conditions are icy it is possible to descend on the French side of the col and traverse around the base of the Cabottes Ridge and reclimb the steep glacier slopes to the saddle.

From the saddle ascend the crevassed glacier northwards skirting the spur of the Aiguille des Glaciers to the L and climb steeply to reach the Dôme de Neige, 3592m.

Now climb towards the summit rocks making for a couloir leading to a notch left of the summit. It is usual to leave skis here. Climb the couloir for c.150m before exiting on the right to follow a snowy rock arête to the summit.

Return, by the route of ascent, to the Dôme de Neige. The descent route now follows the south-west ridge of the Aiguille des Glaciers. Descend this as far as the small gap known as the Col Moyen Age. Continue descending the rocky ridge, which is best done on foot. This leads to the Col des Glaciers, a broad saddle on the ridge marked by two large rocks.

The initial descent to the NW is very steep and crosses several bergschrunds, which later in the season are likely to be open. It may be best to descend on foot until more reasonable slopes make skiing the preferred option. Descend the glacier bay N directly towards the Refuge des Conscrits. Cross the Glacier Tré-la-Tête and climb to the hut.

Stage 7
Conscrits Hut, 2730m – Dômes de Miage, 3670m – les Contamines Montjoie, 1467m

Ascent:	900m to pt.3633m
Descent:	2400m
Difficulty:	BSA. PD.
Principal Aspect:	SE in ascent W in descent
Time:	8 hours

This is a splendid summit on which to end the tour and one that is frequently climbed on skis. The first ski ascent was made by de Gemmes, Feberey, Fleuth and Sexauer in May 1926.

There are several options possible. From the Col des Dômes, pt.3633m can be reached on skis. A traverse as far as the Col de la Bérangère can be made on foot, and a descent on skis from there made to the hut. Many skiers, however, make a ski depot at pt.3633m, climb to the main summit on foot, return to the depot and descend by the route of ascent.

From the hut gain the Tré-la-Tête glacier and begin climbing NE towards the Col Infranchissable. Pass below pt.3169m at the toe of the ridge, descending from pt.3633m of the Dômes de Miage still in the direction of the col before bearing left into the glacial bay below the Col des Dômes. A line of crevasses is normally turned on the right, and the col is reached after a final steep climb. The arête is then followed to the L as far as pt.3633m. From a ski depot a traverse of the Dômes de Miage can be made on foot, to and from pt.3670m. Descend by the route of ascent to the hut.

It is also possible to traverse as far as the Col de la Bérangère and make a steep descent down a well-defined gully on foot before skiing directly to the Conscrits Hut.

The descent to the Hotel Tré-la-Tête follows the right bank of the Tré-la-Tête Glacier. At its snout leave it on the R, making a slight climb before traversing horizontally, crossing the 'Mauvais Pas', to pt.2096m. This difficult step is a band of steep slabby rocks above a considerable drop. Great care is needed crossing it, but it can be rope protected. Descend to the Hotel Tré-la-Tête. Continue N through forest to the Maison Forestière before crossing the Grande Combe and descending again on a forest track to le Cugnon. Late in the season you will be lucky to find skiable snow on this section. It is then a short walk to the fleshpots of Contamines.

Glacier d'Armancette

Ascent:	1015m
Descent:	2370m
Difficulty:	BSA. AD+ – D. Good conditions essential especially in the lower part of the route before Lac Armancette.
Principal Aspect:	SE in ascent. NW, N in descent.
Time:	6 hours from the hut

This is a more difficult alternative to descending the Tré-la-Tête Glacier to Contamines. The Glacier d'Armancette is a huge glacier slope, which in good conditions offers a magnificent, not too difficult, yet classic descent of over 2000m. The route is complex and combines all the difficulties and dangers of high Alpine terrain. One must be prepared for variable snow conditions that inevitably exist between a high summit and deep valley. Once off the glacier the difficulties continue with a steep couloir and ever-present menace of serac and stonefall. Amazingly it was first ski descended in 1937 by J. Dieterlen. It is essential to have good conditions in the Vallon Covagnet.

From the summit of the Dômes de Miage, pt.3670m, it is possible to descend the Glacier d'Armancette directly. This is bold and steep (S4/S5) and should not be considered in icy conditions. The descent follows the glacier's steep right bank in a sweep around a rock spur to a flatter plateau area at c.3000m. A less bold start is to descend the Glacier d'Armancette from near the Col de la Bérangère to a glacier plateau at c.3000m.

Most opt to descend from the summit towards the Col de la Bérangère (S4), from where a diagonal descent rightwards crosses between crevasses towards the glacier's right bank and a plateau area at c.2900m. Leave the glacier by going right to reach a small col and descend superb N-facing slopes to below the Pointe de Covagnet. Descend W in a steep combe, the Vallon Covagnet, by its right bank beneath the Covagnet ridge as far as 2500m. Then follow a short, steep couloir (S4) going R to c.2000 and a narrow ramp, which in turn leads to the Lac d'Armancette (usually under snow). Follow the right bank of the stream issuing from the lake, gradually bearing N to La Frasse above Contamines.

MONT BLANC HAUTE ROUTE: USEFUL INFORMATION

Huts

Argentière Hut. Tel: 50 53 16 92. 24 places in winter

Trient Hut. Tel: (res) 02 77 22 91 58. Tel (hut): 02 77 83 14 38

Montenvers Hut (private), 1913m. Tel: 04 50 53 00 33

Requin Hut. Tel: 50 53 16 96

Cosmiques Hut, 3613m. Tel: 04 50 54 40 16

Goûter Hut, 3800m. Tel: 04 50 54 40 93

Gonella Hut. Tel: 0039 165 885 101

Grands Mulets, 3052m. Tel: 04 50 53 16 98

Robert Blanc Hut, 2750m. Tel: 04 79 07 24 22/04 79 07 79 79

Conscrits Hut, 2580m. Tel: 04 50 47 76 70/01 53 72 87 11

Hotel Tré-la-Tête (private), 1970m. Tel: 04 50 47 01 68

Useful Contacts

Champex Tourist Office. Tel: 027/783 12 27

Martigny Tourist Office. Tel: 27/721 22 24

Argentière Tourist Office. Tel: 04 50 53 00 24

Chamonix Tourist Office. Tel: 04 50 53 00 24

Contamines Tourist Office. Tel: 04 50 47 01 58

Office de la Haute Montagne in Chamonix. Tel: 53 23 22 08

Cont. over page

Chamonix – Aiguille du Midi cable car. Tel: 50.53.30.80

Argentière – Grands Montets cable car. Tel: 50.54.00.82

Weather Information

Avalanche Bulletin Haute Savoie. Tel: 08 36 68 02 74

Chamonix Meteo. Tel: 450 53 17 11

www.chamonix-meteo.com

www.chamonix-weather.com

Six-day weather forecast in English. Tel: 08 92 70 03 30

Emergency and Rescue

PGHM in Chamonix. Tel: 50 53 16 89

PGHM St Gervais. Tel: 04 50 78 10 81

Police Emergency, France. Tel 112

Police Emergency, Italy. Tel: 113

Skinning towards the Col de Bérard

HIGH-LEVEL DAY-TOURS IN THE MONT BLANC MASSIF

I make no apologies for including a selection of high-level day-tours around the Mont Blanc massif. It is generally accepted that Mont Blanc, with Chamonix as a focal point, is the centre of world Alpinism. Its mountains act as a magnet to mountaineers and extreme sports specialists from all over the world. The skiing is pretty good too. Some even suggest that the Grands Montets is the best single off-piste ski hill in the world – although there are those who might want to argue that point. The fact is that with a vertical interval of over 2000m, a long season and three sides to the mountain offering couloirs, glaciers, open slopes, drop-offs and much more it is certainly up there vying for centre place on the podium. On the other hand, few would dispute that the Vallée Blanche is the most famous off-piste ski run in the Alps – it is certainly the most crowded.

What is clear-cut is that the mountains that make up the Mont Blanc range offer some magnificent ski mountaineering in a quite awesome setting. The peaks, passes and glaciers of the area are amongst the most spectacular and well known in the Alps. That the area offers magnificent day-tours seems, at first, to be at odds with the size and savagery of the terrain. Mechanical uplift provides the answer; cable cars offer fast and efficient access into places that would otherwise be inaccessible as day-tours. It is not just the main range that provides the action. On the north side of the Chamonix valley the dramatic pinnacled crest of the Aiguilles Rouge is a paradise for both touring and off-piste skiing. Once again the lift system, not huts, is the answer to access. That said, some day-tours are best done from mountain huts, making the whole thing a much more leisurely and, some would suggest, enjoyable pursuit. In fact huts like the Argentière, Trient, Requin, Conscrits, Cosmiques and others provide superb bases from which to make tours.

I've included a selection of my favourite day-tours in this guidebook because, sooner or later, most ski tourers visit the Mont Blanc region, either to start the High Level Route or to ski Mont Blanc. Few go there for hut-to-hut tours, although the Mont Blanc Haute Route I've included is a demanding 'classic'. All the day-tours described are enjoyable in their own right, but they also provide the grounding and acclimatisation for those setting out on a major high-level traverse.

DAY-TOURS IN THE AIGUILLES ROUGE
COL DES AIGUILLES CROCHUES TO LE BUET

Col des Aiguilles Crochues – Col Bérard – Le Buet

Ascent:	500m
Descent:	1550m
Difficulty:	PD+
Principal Aspect:	mainly E and S
Time:	4–5 hours
Starting Point:	Les Praz de Chamonix – Flégère cable car
Best Time:	December–May
Maps:	IGN 1:25,000 Chamonix Massif du Mont Blanc 3630 OT TOP 25

A fine and popular and classic day-tour that provides a good introduction to the Aiguille Rouge, passing through much magnificent scenery in suprisingly remote-feeling surroundings. The views of the Mont Blanc massif from the top of the Index are superb. As with most of the tours in the Chamonix valley a cable car makes this a comfortable day-tour. Without the Flégère and Index lifts you would have an additional 1325m of ascent! Returning to Chamonix or Argentière from Le Buet is simple because the tour ends not only at a good café but also the railway station.

From the village of Les Praz de Chamonix take the cable car to Flégère and then the bubble-car to the Index, 2385m, and finally the highest drag lift. The earliest lift begins at 8.30am, but this may vary. From the top of the lift make an ascending traverse R to gain the Combe des Aiguilles Crochues. There are two Cols des Aiguilles Crochues; the one marked as pt.2701m is the one normally reached on skis. The slope beneath this col is steep, and the last few metres to the col are often more easily done on foot.

From the col make a gently descending traverse N

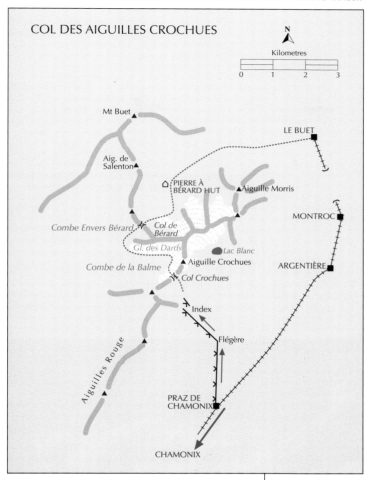

below the Aiguille Crochues and the tiny Glacier des Dards before making a broad sweep W under the buttresses of the Aigille du Belvédère. Stay on the obvious traverse line below the Point Alphonse Favre to reach the

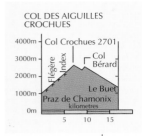

COL DES AIGUILLES
CROCHUES

Combe d'Envers Bérard above pt.2288m. The slope below the Pt Alphonse Favre faces south and is a known avalanche slope. In icy conditions this traverse can feel quite exposed, as the slope falls precipitously to Combe de la Balme. By maintaining a gently descending traverse you should loose minimal height and reach a point where it is possible to see the Col Bérard.

Once you turn the corner into the Combe d'Envers Bérard it is time to put skins back on and make the relatively gentle ascent to the Col de Bérard, 2460m. From the col the deep Bérard valley extends NE, offering a splendid descent beginning with a series of enjoyable pitches into the Combe de Bérard down its left or right flank – search and it is normally possible to find good snow and a chance for 'fresh tracks'. At c.2179m turn N to gain the main valley below the Refuge de la Pierre à Bérard. The regular descent of the Bérard valley keeps to the right of the stream, although in the upper section of the valley a track sometimes follows the true left bank before crossing to the right bank at la Vordette, 1528m. Below this point the trail invariably provides interesting bushwacking before joining the tiny ski area at La Poya before the road at Le Buet.

Traversing towards the Aiguilles Crochues and the start of the climb to the Col Crochues

COL DU BELVÉDÈRE TO LE BUET
Col du Belvédère, 2780m – Glacier de Bérard – Le Buet

The steep climb to the Col des Aiguilles Crochues

Start:	Les Praz de Chamonix
Finish:	Le Buet
Ascent:	500m from Index; 980m from Flégère
Descent:	1480m
Difficulty:	D-. Another of the classic col crossings for which the Aiguille Rouge are justifiably famous. The descent of the Couloir du Belvédère is the key to the route.
Duration:	5–6 hours
Best Time:	December–May
Maps:	IGN 1:25,000 Chamonix Massif du Mont Blanc 3630 OT TOP 25

Another Aiguille Rouge classic and a highly sought-after tour, although much less often crossed than the Col Crochues. More difficult than the Crochues, the traverse of the Col du Belvédère crosses steeper ground, demands a wider range of skills and usually a rope to descend the Couloir du Belvédère.

From Les Praz de Chamonix take the lift to Flégère and then the bubble to the Index, 2385m, and finally the drag lift. From its high point make a descending traverse NE to gain and descend the Combe des Aiguilles Crochues,

*Magnificent
conditions in the
Aiguille Rouge –
below the Col Cornu*

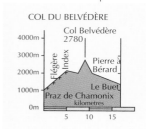

making for an obvious shoulder (c.2300m) on the long south-east ridge of the Aiguille Crochues. It is normally possible to reach the shoulder without skinning, although it is sometimes necessary to side-step a little to reach it. In icy conditions this is a bad place to slip. Once round the shoulder continue to Lac Blanc, 2352m.

Lac Blanc can also be reached by a traverse from the Chalet de la Flégère, adding at least an hour to the ascent, but this may be preferable if the shoulder is icy. From the top of the Flégère cable car descend the piste below the Telesiege de la Trappe before contouring NE towards pt.1764m and then climbing more steeply N in the direction of Lac Blanc.

Traverse around the E side of the Lac Blanc, ascending NW into the Combe du Belvédère before climbing directly, and steeply in several places, to the well-marked Col du Belvédère.

On the far side the north-west couloir falls away abruptly to the Glacier de Bérard. The first 100m are particularly steep, and most people descend on foot safeguarded by a rope. Once the glacier has been reached, descend this by its left (W) bank to gain the Combe de Bérard and continue to the main valley below the Refuge de la Pierre à Bérard. The normal descent of the Bérard valley keeps to the right of the stream, although in the upper section of the valley a track sometimes follows the true left bank

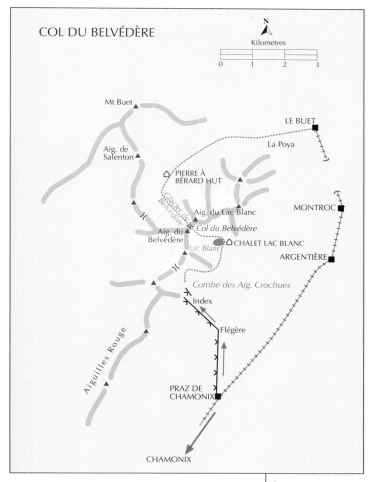

COL DU BELVÉDÈRE

before crossing to the right bank at la Vordette, 1528m. Below this point the trail invariably provides interesting bushwacking before joining the tiny ski area at La Poya before the road at Le Buet.

COL DE BEAUGENT TO LE BUET

Col de Beaugeant, 2807m – Bérard valley – Le Buet

Start:	Les Praz de Chamonix
Finish:	Le Buet – Vallorcine
Ascent:	470m from the Index; 935m from Flégère
Descent:	1457m
Difficulty:	AD. The final 50m to the col are often delicate and icy, but can be protected by rope. Pegs in place. The descent is steep in places. Difficult route-finding in poor visibility. An early start is essential.
Duration:	5 hours
Best Time:	December–May
Maps:	IGN 1:25,000 Chamonix Massif du Mont Blanc 3630 OT TOP 25

A magnificent col, perhaps the finest in the trilogy described, although a little easier than the Col du Belvédère. It combines a technically interesting ascent with a steep descent in a remote setting. One of the most satisfying crossings in the Aiguilles Rouge. It is a good idea to take the earliest cable car as the ascent slope is south facing.

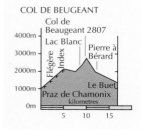

COL DE BEUGENT

The first task is to reach Lac Blanc. From Les Praz de Chamonix take the cable car and bubble lift to the Index top station, 2385m. From there make a gently descending traverse NE to cross the Combe des Aiguilles Crochues. Having crossed this hollow bear SE, making for an obvious shoulder (c.2300m) on the long SE ridge of the Aiguille Crochues. It is normally possible to reach the shoulder without skinning, although it is sometimes necessary to side-step a little to reach it. In icy conditions this is a bad place to slip. Once round the shoulder continue to Lac Blanc, 2352m.

Lac Blanc can also be reached by a traverse from the Chalet de la Flégère, adding at least an hour to the ascent, but this may be preferable if the shoulder is icy. From the top of the Flégère cable car descend the piste below the Telesiege de la Trappe before contouring NE towards pt.1764m and then climbing steeply N in the direction of Lac Blanc.

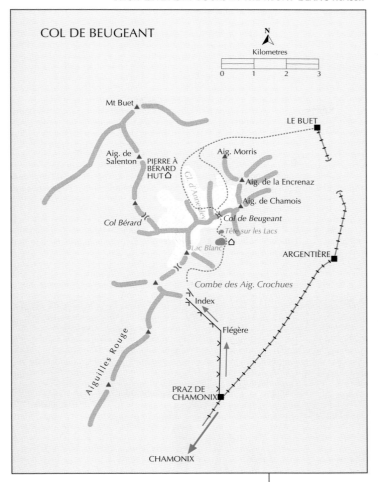

From Lac Blanc ascend NNW towards the Tête sur les Lacs. Pass W of the small lake and so gain the snowy cirque leading to Col de Beugeant. The snow steepens dramatically as you near the col. As you ascend, aim for a point below the pinnacled ridge 50m to the right of the col. From this point skis are carried. A rising traverse is then made, usually over ice-glazed rocks, to reach the Col de Beugeant. It is possible to protect the traverse with a rope (pegs usually in place). Be aware that this slope faces south and gets the sun early.

From the narrow col you have two options.

Option 1: Descend to the R passing just below the rocky spur of the Aiguille de Chamois. Continue NE down the Glacier de Beugeant in the direction of the Col de l'Encrenaz. Instead of gaining the col, bear L to descend the right bank of the glacier, passing below the west flank of the Aiguille Morris. At c.2000m, two descent possibilities present themselves. Either make a steep traverse to the left to reach a steep couloir/stream bed, which can be descended directly to pt.1702m in the Bérard valley. Or, at c.2000m, traverse to the R until below the Aiguille de Mesure, before making a diagonal descent to pt.1702m.

Option 2: The alternative descent from the Col de Beugeant is via the Glacier d'Anneuley and is slightly

On the traverse between the Index and Lac Blanc en route to the Col Beugeant

easier. From the col go down to the R passing below the rocky spur descending from the Aiguille de Chamois. Then descend NW to c.2550m and cross the north ridge of the Aiguille Tête Plate at a shoulder marked as le Chardonnet and so gain the Glacier d'Anneuley. Continue on a descending traverse to the W before easier slopes lead to the Bérard valley below the Bérard Refuge. Descend the valley to Le Buet.

The normal descent of the Bérard valley keeps to the right of the stream, although in the upper section of the valley a track sometimes follows the true left bank before crossing to the right bank at la Vordette, 1528m. Below this point the trail invariably provides interesting bushwacking before joining the tiny ski area at La Poya and the road at Le Buet.

Ascending steep slopes below the Col Beugeant – the final rocky scramble leads to the snowy notch on the left

DAY-TOURS FROM THE GRANDS MONTETS OR ARGENTIÈRE HUT

The Grands Montets provides a magnificent springboard for a large number of tours and outstanding off-piste runs. Given that you can get an early lift to the top it provides the ideal starting point for all of these tours. Alternatively, for those who prefer a high Alpine ambience and the benefit of an early, unhurried start, the Argentière Hut provides the answer. It is easily reached from the Grands Montets top lift.

Below the Argentière Hut

COL DU TOUR NOIR, 3535m

Ascent:	760m from the Refuge d'Argentière
Descent:	760 to the refuge; 2335m to Argentière
Difficulty:	SAM. PD.
Principal Aspect:	SW
Duration:	5 hours from the Grands Montets; 2–3 hours in ascent from the refuge
Best Time:	February–May
Maps:	IGN 1:25,000 Chamonix Massif du Mont Blanc 3630 OT TOP 25

From the refuge climb NW up steep slopes keeping to the hollow (mulde) between the lateral moraine of the

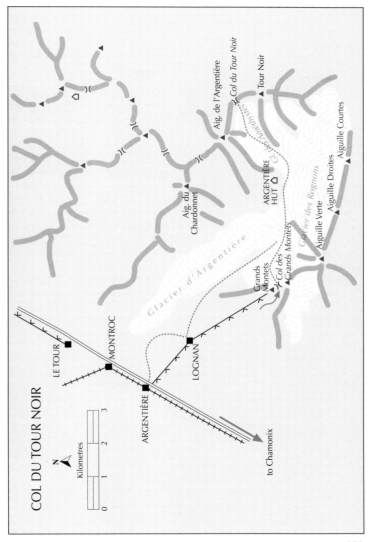

COL DU TOUR NOIR

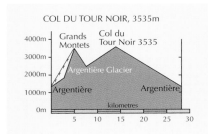

COL DU TOUR NOIR, 3535m

Glacier des Améthystes and the SW Arête of the Aiguille d'Argentière, and so gain the Glacier des Améthystes via a short, steep ascent at c.3000m. Keep well left of a zone of seracs and crevasses whilst continuing to ascend the true right bank of the glacier that leads, finally, to Col du Tour Noir, 3535m.

A popular and scenically beautiful tour amongst high peaks and snaking glaciers set deep in the heart of the Argentière glacier basin. The ascent of the Col du Tour Noir can be completed as a day-tour from the Grands Montets, given that you manage to get the earliest 'ben' – alternatively, an overnight stay at the Argentière Hut will ensure an early start and, ideally, a sunrise seen from the col!

Be aware as you pass beneath the impressive 'Y Couloir' of the Aiguille d'Argentière that this is a known avalanche chute.

Most skiers descend from the col by their route of ascent certainly as far as the hut. From the hut continue down the Glacier d'Argentière crossing to the foot of the rognon below the Grands Montets, c.2550m. At this point off-piste routes from the Grands Montets merge with the glacier.

Alternatively, it is possible to ski directly down the middle of the Glacier des Améthystes to its junction with the Glacier d'Argentière and then continue down the Glacier d'Argentière to the foot of the rognon below the Grands Montets, c.2550m. From this point both routes follow the same course.

Carry on down the true left bank of the glacier in the depression between it and the rocks of the rognon. This can sometimes be quite narrow, with awkward drop-offs and icy patches. The glacier is rejoined where it flattens, and is followed down its left bank (invariably a piste) until it is possible to cross the moraine at c.2338m at a point where the glacier becomes a jumble of seracs. Having crossed the moraine join the Point de Vue piste from the Grands Montets leading to la Croix de Lognan, 1973m, from where a piste leads to Argentière. It is also possible to descend more directly to Argentière via the Refuge de Lognan.

AIGUILLE D'ARGENTIÈRE, 3902m, VIA THE GLACIER DU MILIEU

Ascent:	1130m from the Refuge d'Argentière
Descent:	1130m to the refuge; 2702m to Argentière
Difficulty:	BSA. D section of S3/4 leading to the summit
Principal Aspect:	SW
Duration:	4–5 hours in ascent
Best Time:	February–May
Maps:	IGN 1:25,000 Chamonix Massif du Mont Blanc 3630 OT TOP 25

Although it is normal to make the ascent from the Argentière Refuge, thus ensuring an early start, many fit and acclimatised parties manage to do the round trip from the valley in a day by using the earliest lift to the Grands Montets. It goes without saying that a good weather forecast is essential.

From the refuge descend W a short way towards the Glacier d'Argentière before turning NW to cross a steep moraine and gain a mulde alongside the Glacier du Milieu. Stay in this hollow and climb steeply towards the

The Aiguille d'Argentière is an exceptional ski-mountaineering day in a superb position, offering stunning views of the Aiguilles Courtes, Droites, Verte and the other great mountains that surround the Argentière Glacier. The ascent and descent of the Aiguille d'Argentière demands both skiing and mountaineering skill in equal measure. The final slope to the summit (350m) is steep and and often icy. It is usually quicker and safer to crampon up this slope to the summit. The Glacier du Milieu is a wonderfully narrow ribbon of ice captured between the pinnacled twin rock ridges of the main peak – the scenery is outstanding.

Looking up the Glacier Milieu on the Aiguille d'Argentière – the col right of the main peak is the Col Tour Noir

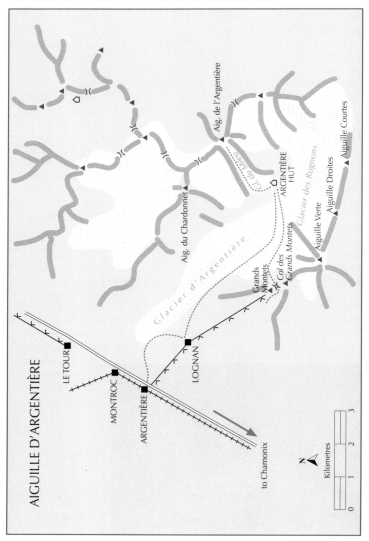

AIGUILLE D'ARGENTIÈRE

LE TOUR

MONTROC

ARGENTIÈRE

LOGNAN

to Chamonix

Aig. de l'Argentière

Aig. du Chardonnet

Col du Chardonnet

ARGENTIÈRE HUT

Glacier des Rognons

Aiguille Courtes

Aiguille Droites

Aiguille Verte

Grands Montets

Col des Grands Montets

Glacier d'Argentière

N

Kilometres

0   1   2   3

snout of the glacier. Having gained the end of the glacier traverse towards its true right bank (N) and climb to *c*.3250m. Now continue more or less up the centre of this narrow, crevassed and imposing glacier to the foot of the final steep slope, *c*.3700m. It is normal to leave skis at this point. Cross the normally large bergschrund, and crampon up the final slope between the two summits of the mountain to reach the crest of the ridge. Turn right and follow the arête to the main summit, pt.3902m.

AIGUILLE D'ARGENTIÈRE, 3902m

Aiguille d'Argentière 3902

Grands Montets

Argentière Glacier

Argentière

Argentière

kilometres

4000m
3000m
2000m
1000m
0m

5   10   15   20   25   30

If the snow conditions are good the descent from the summit can be excellent, albeit steep. In which case, instead of making a ski depot, you may wish to carry your skis to the summit, from which an exciting descent awaits you. In icy or difficult conditions this steep slope is precarious and requires great care – it has been the scene of many falls. Once below the bergschrund continue via the route of ascent as far as the refuge or the Glacier d'Argentière.

Continue down the Glacier d'Argentière crossing to the foot of the rognon below the Grands Montets,

A large snow cornice along the summit ridge of the Aiguille d'Argentière

c.2550m. At this point routes from the Grands Montets merge with the glacier. Carry on down the true left bank of the glacier in a valley between it and the rocks of the rognon. The glacier is rejoined where it flattens until finally it is possible to cross the moraine at c.2338m, at which point the glacier on the right becomes a jumble of seracs. Having crossed the moraine join the Point de Vue piste from the Grands Montets, which leads to la Croix de Lognan lift station, 1973m. It is also possible to descend directly to Argentière via the Refuge de Lognan.

THE THREE COLS

Col du Chardonnet, 3323m – Fenêtre de Saleina, 3267m – Col du Tour, 3282m

Start:	Argentière – Grands Montets cable car
Finish:	Le Tour
Ascent:	1050m
Descent:	2370m
Difficulty:	PD+. A serious high-level traverse on glaciers throughout. Stable conditions and good weather essential. Abseil descent from the Col du Chardonnet normal.
Duration:	7–10 hours; 6–8 from the Argentière Refuge
Best Time:	February–May
Maps:	IGN 1:25,000 Chamonix Massif du Mont Blanc 3630 OT TOP 25

This is a valley classic, truly one of the great day-tours. Throughout the the day the scenery is magnificent with huge glaciers, serac barriers, steep cols and vast ice-hung mountain walls in all directions. Although this covers the greater part of the first day of the Haute Route it is not a route to get fit on. To enjoy it fully you need to be acclimatised and moving well. Only then will a party have little trouble completing the route in a day from the earliest lift to the Grands Montets. Otherwise an overnight in the Argentière Refuge is advisable, as this ▼

From the Col des Grands Montets (this could be regarded as a fourth col, but if you arrive by lift it doesn't count). Descend to the Argentière Glacier right of the obvious rognon as you look towards the glacier Argentière. Traverse the glacier towards the south-west ridge of the Aiguille d'Argentière and ascend the

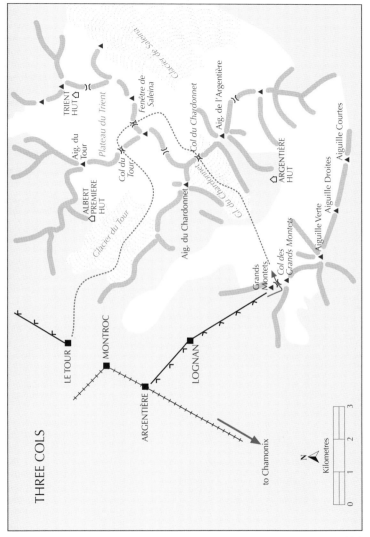

THREE COLS

TRIENT HUT

Aig. du Tour

ALBERT PREMIÈRE HUT

Glacier du Tour

Glacier de Saleina

Plateau du Trient

Fenêtre de Saleina

Col du Tour

Col du Chardonnet

Aig. de l'Argentière

ARGENTIÈRE HUT

Aiguille Courtes

Aiguille Droites

Col du Chardonnet

Aig. du Chardonnet

Aiguille Verte

Col des Grands Montets

Grands Montets

LE TOUR

MONTROC

ARGENTIÈRE

LOGNAN

to Chamonix

N

THREE COLS

Kilometres

0   1   2   3

▲ makes an early start possible. Flagging parties have been known to overnight at the Trient Hut!

One thing is certain, good visibility and snow conditions are essential. You can expect to encounter a wide range of snow conditions, as the tour covers every slope aspect.

Glacier du Chardonnet usually by its true left bank. Depending on conditions, climb either the rocky lower slopes of the south-west ridge or steeply up the glacier right of centre, keeping clear of the main icefall. Above the icefall at c.2800m it is usually possible to traverse into the centre of the glacier. At this point the climbing angle eases as the route finds a way through a zone of crevasses. Continue directly and less steeply to the Col du Chardonnet, 3323m (the first col). This is an impressive place with stunning views of the ice-hung north flanks of the Aiguilles Verte and Droites.

From the col descend the narrow couloir on the north-east side for about 80m. The bergschrund at the foot of the couloir is usually gained by an abseil or steep down climbing. In good conditions the bold opt to sideslip or ski the couloir, but other parties below may make this impossible or unsafe.

From the bergschrund make a gently descending traverse NE around the Saleina Glacier passing below pt.3084. This is the foot of the rocky spur descending from the Grand Fourche. In clear weather it should be possible to make out the narrow gap of the Fenêtre de Saleina, 3267m, the second col, at the head of the basin between the Petite Fourche and the Aiguille de la Fenêtre and Aiguilles Dorées. Skin towards the notch, ascending gradually to a point more or less below it. The last 30m are steep and often best climbed on foot. This is stunning place, with dramatic views of the Aiguille d'Argentière's north face.

From the Fenêtre traverse NW below the Aiguille de la Fenêtre and Tête Blanche, and climb easily to the Col du Tour, 3282m (the third col). Descend quite steeply on the W side before bearing SW towards pt.3238m, below the north face of the imposing

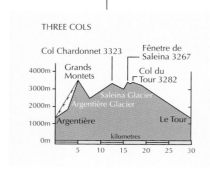

THREE COLS

Col Chardonnet 3323

Fênetre de Saleina 3267

Grands Montets

Col du Tour 3282

4000m
3000m
2000m
1000m
0m

Saleina Glacier

Argentière Glacier

Argentière

Le Tour

kilometres

5 10 15 20 25 30

Aiguille du Chardonnet, continuing to c.3100m below the Aigiuille du Passon. At this point turn NW to gain the broad slopes below the N side the Col du Passon.

Descsend N and then NW across the Glacier du Tour towards a distinctive rock ridge, pt.2722m, making sure to keep well left of the seracs. Now descend the steep glacier slopes between pt.2722m and the Bec Rouge inferior, gradually bearing left. Continue descending, and at c.2300m cross to the left side of a distinctive moraine to pass below the rocks of the Bec de la Cluy, 2334m. Keep traversing to the left before descending the steep north-facing slopes N below the Tête du Grand Chantet, 1967m. These steep, open slopes of the Montagne de Peclerey lead in turn to forested slopes, at which point you bear R towards Le Tour, keeping out of the trees on an open slope. At c.1600m, where the slope steepens, make a descending traverse L avoiding a rocky barrier until the angle once again eases and it is possible to descend without difficulty to Le Tour.

Below the north-west face of the Aiguille d'Argentière during a traverse of the Three Cols

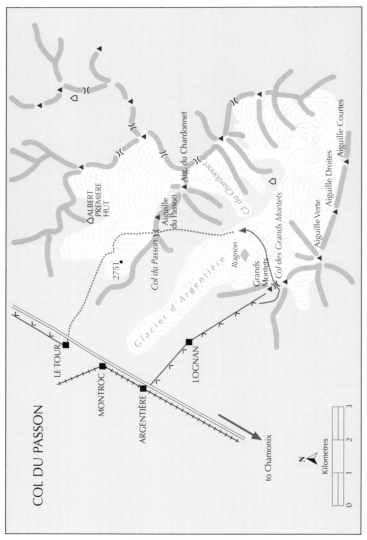

COL DU PASSON

ALBERT PREMIÈRE HUT

Aiguille du Passon

Aig. du Chardonnet

Col du Chardonnet

Col du Passon

2751

Glacier d'Argentière

Rognon

Grands Montets

Col des Grands Montets

Aiguille Verte

Aiguille Droites

Aiguille Courtes

LE TOUR

MONTROC

ARGENTIÈRE

LOGNAN

to Chamonix

N

Kilometres

0   1   2   3

COL DU PASSON, 3028m

Ascent:	730m
Descent:	2500m
Difficulty:	BSA. D-. The final approach to the Col du Passon is steep and exposed.
Principal Aspect:	SW in ascent. NW in descent.
Duration:	5–6 hours
Starting Point:	Grands Montets
Best Time:	February–May
Maps:	IGN 1:25,000 Chamonix Massif du Mont Blanc 3630 OT TOP 25

The Col du Passon is a popular, albeit demanding, ascent requiring sound technique and solid skills. Made fashionable because of easy access from the Grands Montets top lift. An early start and good visibility are recommended for this tour. Finding the best descent to the village of Le Tour is not easy, and there are many options with steep couloirs and rocky barriers. There is also considerable avalanche hazard between the Bec de la Cluy and the Tête des Cascades. In good conditions, however, it provides a great day and is rightly a valley classic.

From the top of the Grands Montets cable car descend to the Col des Grands Montets. The col provides a perfect balcony from which to reconnoitre the line of the ascent and if no trace is in place to chart the route.

From the Col des Grands Montets descend right of the rognon to gain the Glacier d'Argentière. Now traverse towards its right bank in the direction of the Glacier du Chardonnet, staying well above a heavily crevassed zone. Having crossed the glacier turn N to join steep slopes below the toe of the Aiguille du Chardonnet. Now make an ascending traverse NW across steep slopes below the Glacier Adams Reilly. Continue on an ascending traverse below the Aiguille du Chardonnet, climbing towards the base of the couloirs that lead to the Col du Passon. Climb the abrupt right-hand couloir on foot, continuing up the steep slopes that eventually lead to the col.

From the col descend, at first N and then NW, across the Glacier du Tour towards a distinctive rock ridge, pt.2722m, making sure to keep well left of the seracs. Now

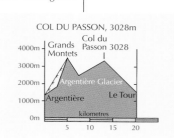

COL DU PASSON, 3028m

descend the steep glacier slopes between pt.2722m and the Bec Rouge inferior, gradually bearing left. Continue descending, and at *c.*2300m cross to the left side of a distinctive moraine to pass below the rocks of the Bec de la Cluy, 2334m. Keep on traversing to the left before descending the steep slopes facing N below the Tête du Grand Chantet, 1967m. These, the steep, open slopes of the Montagne de Peclerey, lead in turn to forested slopes, at which point you bear R towards Le Tour, keeping out of the trees on an open slope. At *c.*1600m, where

Climbing steep glacier terrain below the Col Tour Noir

the slope steepens, make a descending traverse L avoiding a rocky barrier until the angle once again eases and it is possible to descend more easily to Le Tour.

MONT BLANC, 4807m, VIA THE GRANDS MULETS

Day One

Ascent:	Day 1 – 741m; Day 2 – 1756m
Descent:	2497m
Difficulty:	AD. A strenuous expedition through serious glacier terrain demanding solid mountaineering and skiing skills, good fitness and acclimatisation.
Principal Aspect:	mainly N
Duration:	A two-day expedition. Day 1 – 4 hours; Day 2 – 10–11 hours

Take the cable car as far as the Plan des Aiguilles, 2233m. The normal traverse line on skis is higher than the normal summer walking path. From the cable-car station traverse the Glacier des Pélerins at c.2385m and climb towards the north spur of the Aiguille du Midi before traversing W and then SW above the ruined Gare des Glaciers at 2414m. Be aware that the slope below the Aiguille du Midi and Glacier Rond presents some stonefall danger once the sun is on it. Continue the traverse SW more or less horizontally to gain the Bossons Glacier at c.2540m. The traverse of the Bossons crosses the relatively flat Plan Glacier before climbing S through the chaos of the Jonction below the Grands Mulets Refuge. This is an area of large crevasses and seracs, and in some conditions can be time consuming

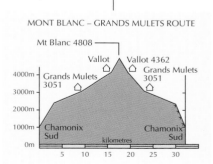

MONT BLANC – GRANDS MULETS ROUTE

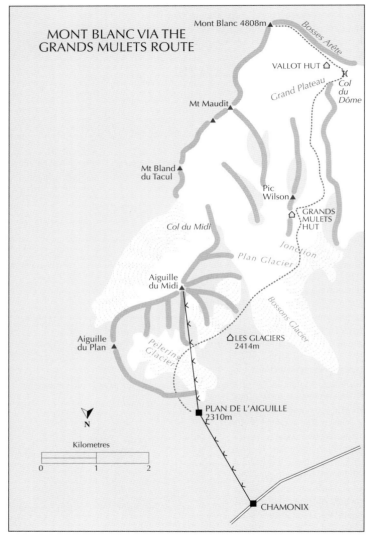

MONT BLANC VIA THE
GRANDS MULETS ROUTE

Mont Blanc 4808m ▲

Bosses Arête

VALLOT HUT ⌂

✕

*Col
du
Dôme*

Grand Plateau

Mt Maudit ▲

Mt Bland
du Tacul ▲

Pic
Wilson ▲

⌂ GRANDS
MULETS
HUT

Col du Midi

Junction

Plan Glacier

Aiguille
du Midi ▲

Bossons Glacier

Aiguille
du Plan ▲

*Pelerin
Glacier*

⌂ LES GLACIERS
2414m

N

Kilometres

0   1   2

■ PLAN DE L'AIGUILLE
2310m

■ CHAMONIX

especially when roped. Continue up the relatively steep snow slope close to the Grands Mulets rognon to its right-hand end below the hut. The final rock buttress leading to the Grands Mulets Refuge, 3051m, has a fixed cable running right to left.

Day Two

Starting Point:	Aiguille du Midi cable car in Chamonix Sud
Best Time:	April–June
Maps:	IGN 1:25,000 Chamonix Massif du Mont Blanc 3630 OT TOP 25

From the refuge traverse SW from the hut and climb initially up the left bank of the glacier below the impressive seracs of the North Arête (Arête Royal) of the Dôme du Goûter. The seracs on the R present considerable avalanche danger and are best avoided by keeping as far L (E) as is practical, and so gain the Petit Plateau. Continue more steeply up the slopes of the Grandes Montées, again avoiding the obvious serac danger on the R, to gain the impressive glacier basin of the Grand Plateau. At c.3960 ascend more steeply SW, passing through several

Mont Blanc via the Grands Mulets is a magnificent two-day expedition to the highest summit in Western Europe. An outstanding ski-mountaineering challenge that was first skied as early as 1904 by Ugo Mylius with the Swiss guides Maurer, Tannler and Zurfluh. In the summer, the Grands Mulets route is a long slog both in ascent and descent. On skis the ascent is no shorter but the descent can be a delight, although not without obvious crevasse and serac danger. In poor visibility route-finding can be difficult. It goes without saying that sound ski-mountaineering skill and good acclimatisation are essential for safety and enjoyment.

View down the Bosses Arête of Mont Blanc towards the Vallot Hut, with the broad slopes of the Dôme du Goûter beyond

crevasse zones, towards the Col du Dôme. Once at this broad col bear left towards the Refuge Vallot, 4362m. Most people make a ski depot here before continuing up the Bosses Arête on foot, which in places can be both steep and narrow.

From the summit return to the Vallot Hut and descend by the route of ascent. The traverse back to the Plan des Aiguilles normally involves about 30 minutes of unwelcome ascent.

MONT BLANC DU TACUL, 4248m – NORTH FACE NORMAL ROUTE

Ascent:	700m
Descent:	2350m to Montenvers – even more if there is snow all the way to Chamonix!
Difficulty:	AD with several S3/4 pitches. A major glacier slope with all the dangers of crevasses, seracs and potential avalanche risk. Several large crevasses can prove particularly difficult to cross.
Principal Aspect:	predominantly N
Duration:	5–6 hours from the Midi top station back to the Col du Midi
Starting Point:	Chamonix Sud, Aiguille du Midi téléphérique
Best Time:	March–May
Maps:	IGN 1:25,000 St Gervais les Bains – Mont Blanc 3531 est

Although it is possible to climb Mont Blanc du Tacul, 4248m, direct from the Aiguille du Midi téléphérique, it is also possible to make use of the Cosmiques Refuge at the Col du Midi to gain an earlier start. Combined with the descent of the Vallée Blanche this provides magnificent skiing, with the total descent greatly exceeding the number of metres climbed – always a good feeling.

It is essential to take the earliest possible cable car to the summit of the Midi. From the top station descend the first stage of the Midi-Plan ridge, which is the start to the Vallée Blanche descent. This is normally well pisted and prepared with a rope handrail. Traverse under

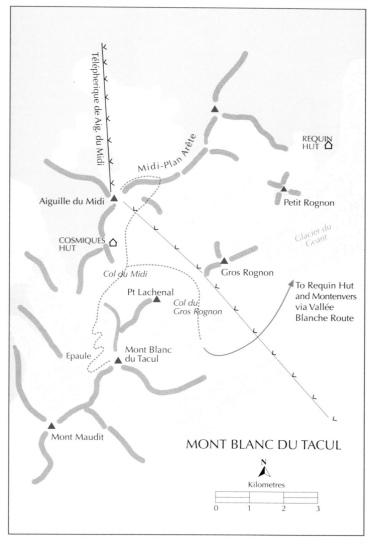

Télépherique de Aig. du Midi

Midi-Plan Arête

REQUIN HUT

Aiguille du Midi

Petit Rognon

Glacier du Géant

COSMIQUES HUT

Gros Rognon

Col du Midi

Pt Lachenal

Col du Gros Rognon

To Requin Hut and Montenvers via Vallée Blanche Route

Epaule

Mont Blanc du Tacul

Mont Maudit

MONT BLANC DU TACUL

N

Kilometres

0   1   2   3

MONT BLANC DU TACUL

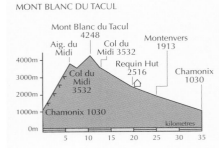

Sarah Fergusson climbing Mont Blanc du Tacul in fine weather but with difficult 'slab' conditions below the shoulder, the result of persistent winds and drifting snow

the beautiful red granite of the Midi's south face buttress to reach the Col du Midi, 3532m. At this point the Vallée Blanche 'piste' turns E to pass between the rocks of the Gros Rognon and the Pointe Lachenal. From the Col the broad shadowy slope of the Mont Blanc du Tacul's north face is well seen, its left-hand margin defined by the rocks and couloirs of the Triangle du Mont Blanc du Tacul.

The slope is in fact a steep glacier, with seracs, crevasses and sometimes a wide bergschrund. Gain the foot of this slope on its left-hand side below a barrier of seracs and quickly make a diagonal traverse R into the centre of the slope. Continue the ascent in a series of steps, sometimes around impressive crevasses and close to a number of seracs. It is often necessary to remove skis

and climb steeper icy sections. The exact route varies from season to season, but the general line, if no track is in place, aims to gain the shoulder of the mountain's west ridge at *c*.4000m. Once gained, this snowy ridge is followed to the final rocky summit pinnacle. It is normal to deposit skis below these rocks and reach the summit on foot.

Descent is normally via the route of ascent, although it is invariably possible to follow a more direct line. It is well worthwhile scouting a good descent line during the ascent, as the face is high and wide with numerous steep pitches with hidden crevasses and seracs.

Once back at the Col du Midi it is normal to descend the main, well-worn descent route of the Vallée Blanche via the Geant Icefall and the Requin Refuge. In poor visibilty, however, this is not advised, in which case it is better to climb back to the Midi and return to Chamonix on the cable car or stay at the refuge.

TOURS FROM THE CONSCRITS HUT

CONTAMINES MONTJOIE TO THE CONSCRITS REFUGE

Contamines Montjoie, 1190m – Hotel Tré-la-Tête, 1970 – Conscrits Refuge, 2730m

Ascent:	1640m
Difficulty:	SAM. Some delicate passages on the ascent to the Tré-la-Tête Hotel.
Principal Aspect:	W
Duration:	5–6 hours
Best Time:	March–May
Maps:	IGN 1:25,000 St Gervais les Bains – Mont Blanc 3531 est

From Contamines follow the forest track via Le Plans, make an ascending of the Grande Combe stream to gain the Maison Forestière. Continue the traverse, crossing

The rebuilt Conscrits Hut provides a magnificent venue for a week of ski mountaineering. High and remote, it has one of the most romantic settings of all the huts in the Mont Blanc range. More than that, it is surrounded by a series of stunning peaks that offer the competent ski mountaineer some demanding tours. The hut itself, once reached, is the ideal base from which to venture on these magnificent mountains.

No easy hut tour this, but a real adventure with considerable technical interest.

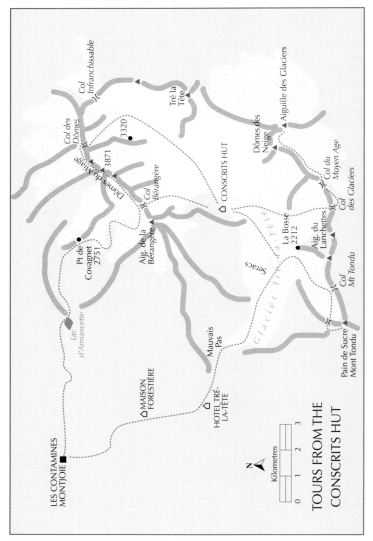

TOURS FROM THE
CONSCRITS HUT

Col Infranchissable

Col des Dômes

Tré la Tête

Aiguille des Glaciers

Dômes des Neige

CONSCRITS HUT

Col du Moyen Age

3320

3871

Dômes du Miage

Col Bérangère

La Tête

Col des Glaciers

Aig. de la Bérangère

La Bosse 2212

Aig. du Lanchettes

Pt de Covagnet 2751

Séracs

Col Mt Tondu

Glacier Tré la Tête

Lac d'Armancette

Pain de Sucre Mont Tondu

Mauvais Pas

MAISON FORESTIÈRE

HOTEL TRÉ-LA-TÊTE

LES CONTAMINES MONTJOIE

N

Kilometres

0   1   2   3

several small gullies before making the final ascent to the Hotel Tré-la-Tête, 1970m. The route now turns E, aiming for the snout of the Tré-la-Tête glacier via the 'mauvais pas' – a difficult slabby step above an impressive drop. However, it can be well protected using a rope. Gain the glacier and follow its right bank passing the Tré la Grande serac barrier. Continue more or less up the right bank until the Conscrits Refuge is visible. When directly S of the hut leave the glacier and reach it directly.

The new hut is comfortable and well positioned for many fine ascents including the Tré-la-Tête and Dômes de Miage.

Descent To Contamines

The descent to the Hotel Tré-la-Tête follows the right bank of the Tré-la-Tête glacier. At its snout leave it on the R, making a slight climb before traversing horizontally, crossing the 'mauvais pas', to pt.2096m. This difficult step is a band of steep slabby rocks above a considerable drop. Great care is needed crossing it, but it can be rope protected. Descend to the Hotel Tré-la-Tête. Continue N through forest to the Maison Forestière before crossing the Grande Combe and descending again on a forest track to le Cugnon. Late in the season you will be lucky to find skiable snow on this section. It is then a short walk to the fleshpots of Contamines.

DÔMES DES MIAGE

Ascent:	900m to pt.3633m
Descent:	900m to the hut or 2400m to Contamines
Difficulty:	SAM. PD.
Principal Aspect:	SE
Duration:	4–5 hours in ascent
Best Time:	March–May
Maps:	IGN 1:25,000 St Gervais les Bains – Mont Blanc 3531 est

This is a splendid summit and one that is frequently climbed on skis. The first ski ascent was made by de Gemmes, Feberey, Fleuth and Sexauer in May 1926. The Glacier d'Armancette, when in condition, provides one of the finest descents in the range.

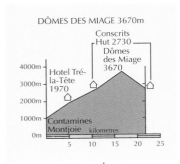

DÔMES DES MIAGE 3670m

There are several options possible. From the Col des Dômes, pt.3633m can be reached on skis. A traverse as far as the Col de la Bérangère can be made on foot, and a descent on ski from there made to the hut. Many opt to make a ski depot at pt.3633m, climb to the main summit on foot, return to the depot and descend on skis by the route of ascent.

From the hut gain the Tré-la-Tête glacier and begin climbing NE towards the Col Infranchissable. Pass below pt.3169m at the toe of the ridge descending from pt.3633m of the Dômes des Miage still in the direction of the col before bearing left into the glacial bay below the Col des Dômes. A line of crevasses is normally turned on the right and the col is reached after a final steep climb. The arête is then followed to the L as far as pt.3633m. From a ski depot a traverse of the Dômes des Miage can be made on foot, to and from pt.3670m. Descend by the route of ascent to the hut.

It is also possible to traverse as far as the Col de la Bérangère and make a steep descent down a well-defined gully on foot before skiing directly to the Conscrits Hut.

Descent by the Glacier d'Armancette

This is a more difficult alternative to descending the Tré-la-Tête glacier to Contamines. The Glacier d'Armancette is a huge glacier slope, which in good conditions offers a magnificent, complex, yet classic descent of over 2000m. The ▶

From the summit of the Dômes de Miage, pt.3670m, it is possible to descend the Glacier d'Armancette directly. This is bold and steep (S4/S5) and should not be considered in icy conditions. The descent follows the glacier's steep right bank in a sweep around a rock spur to a flatter plateau area at c.3000m. (A less bold start is to descend the Glacier d'Armancette from near the Col de la Bérangère to a glacier plateau at c.3000m.)

Most opt to descend from the summit towards the Col de la Bérangère (S4), from where a diagonal descent rightwards crosses between crevasses towards the glacier's right bank and a plateau area at c.2900m.

Ascent:	1015m
Descent:	2370m
Difficulty:	TBSA. Pitches S4. AD+ – D. Good conditions essential, especially in the lower part of the route before Lac Armancette.
Principal Aspect:	SE in ascent. NW, N in descent.
Duration:	4–5 hours in ascent. 6–8 hours total.
Best Time:	March–May
Maps:	IGN 1:25,000 St Gervais les Bains – Mont Blanc 3531 est

Leave the glacier by going right to reach a small col, and descend superb north-facing slopes to below the Pointe de Covagnet. Descend W in a steep combe, the Vallon Covagnet, by its right bank beneath the Covagnet ridge as far as 2500m. Then follow a short, steep couloir (S4) going R to c.2000 and a narrow ramp which in turn leads to the Lac d'Armancette (usually under snow). Follow the right bank of the stream issuing from the lake, gradually bearing N to La Frasse above Contamines.

AIGUILLE DES GLACIERS

Ascent:	1086m
Descent:	1086m
Difficulty:	BSA. AD+ S3/4 on the approach to the Col des Glaciers.
Principal Aspect:	N, SW
Duration:	8–10 hours in total
Best Time:	March–May
Maps:	IGN 1:25,000 St Gervais les Bains – Mont Blanc 3531 est

route is technically interesting and combines all the difficulties and dangers of high Alpine terrain. One must be prepared for the variable snow conditions that inevitably exist between a high summit and low valley. Once off the glacier the difficulties continue with a steep couloir and ever-present menace of serac and stonefall. Amazingly it was first ski descended in 1937 by J. Dieterlen. It is essential to have good conditions in the Vallon Covagnet.

A splendidly remote and fine-looking mountain that provides a technical and strenuous ascent of a mountain that straddles the Franco/Italian frontier.

Descent from the Aiguille du Midi and the start of numerous tours in the Mont Blanc range, including the ever popular Vallée Blanche descent

From the hut descend to the glacier Tré-la-Tête and traverse SW to the glacier bay leading to the Col des Glaciers. Ascend steep slopes in the direction of the Pointes des Lanchettes. The final 100m slope is very steep and there are normally several large crevasses to cross. Carry skis to reach the col, marked by two large rocks, on foot. If the col is the objective a ski depot can be made below the bergschrund.

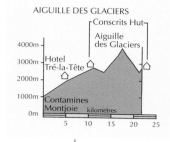

The ascent to the Aiguille des Glaciers continues along the rocky SW ridge (carrying skis). Follow this as far as the small gap marked as the Col Moyen Age. Continue up the now broader ridge, which is steep in places, as far as the Dôme des Neige, 3592m.

Now climb towards the summit rocks making for a couloir leading to a notch left of the summit. It is usual to leave skis here. Climb the couloir for c.150m before exiting on the right for a snowy rock arête leading to the summit.

Descend by the route of ascent to Col des Glaciers and onwards to the Refuge des Conscrits.

PAIN DE SUCRE DU MONT TONDU, 3196m

Ascent:	870m
Descent:	8870m
Difficulty:	BSA. AD. Short section of S3/4 below the summit.
Principal Aspect:	NE in ascent
Duration:	3–4 hours in ascent; 5–7 hours in total
Best Time:	March–May
Maps:	IGN 1:25,000 St Gervais les Bains – Mont Blanc 3531 est

The Pain de Sucre is a classic ascent on this side of the range and is often done from the Hotel Tré-la-Tête. However, it is as well done from the Conscrits Hut. The summit is a magnificent viewpoint and offers a choice of descent routes.

From the hut descend the Glacier Tré-la-Tête to c.2400m, above the seracs Tré la Grande. Traverse the

157

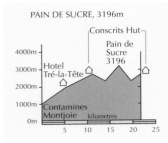

PAIN DE SUCRE, 3196m

glacier in the direction of the Glacier du Mont Tondu aiming for la Bosse at the base of the north-northeast ridge of the Aiguille des Lanchettes. Make a diagonal ascent R from the base of la Bosse des Lanchettes up steep slopes to reach the Glacier du Mont Tondu. Continue up the glacier towards the Col du Mont Tondu. From below the col begin making a diagonal ascent rightwards to reach the col on the ridge connecting the Mont Tondu and the Pyramid Chaplan, 3035m. Follow the ridge S to the summit.

In descent it is possible to retrace your route to the col and descend the route of ascent. Alternatively, it is possible to ski down the steep northern flank from the summit (S4) and thereby descend the route of ascent to the Conscrits Hut.

It is also possible to descend the west face of the Pain de Sucre du Mont Tondu, 3196m, via Lake Jovet and thereby return to Contamines. This is more difficult.

MONT BLANC DAY-TOURS: USEFUL INFORMATION

Huts

Argentière Hut. Tel: 50 53 16 92.
24 places in winter

Trient Hut. Tel: 02 77 83 14 38

Montenvers Hut (private), 1913m.
Tel: 04 50 53 00 33

Requin Hut. Tel: 50 53 16 96

Cosmiques Hut, 3613m.
Tel: 04 50 54 40 16

Goûter Hut, 3800m.
Tel: 04 50 54 40 93

Grands Mulets, 3052m.
Tel: 04 50 53 16 98

Conscrits Hut, 2580m.
Tel: 04 50 47 76 70/
01 53 72 87 11

Hotel Tré-la-Tête (private),
1970m. Tel: 04 50 47 01 68

Useful Contacts

Argentière Tourist Office.
Tel: 04 50 54 02 14

Chamonix Tourist Office.
Tel: 04 50 53 00 24

Contamines Tourist Office.
Tel: 04 50 47 01 58

Chamonix – Aiguille du Midi
cable car. Tel: 50.53.30.80

Argentière – Grands Montets
cable car. Tel: 50.54.00.82

La Praz – Flégère cable car.
Tel : 50.53.18.58

Office de la Haute Montagne in
Chamonix. Tel: 53 23 22 08

Office de Haute Montagne. Tel:
04 50 53 22 08. email: ohm-
info@chamonix.com

Weather Information

Avalanche Bulletin Haute Savoie.
Tel: 08 36 68 02 74/
08 36 68 10 20

Chamonix Meteo.
Tel: 450 53 17 11

Six-day weather forecast in
English. Tel: 08 92 70 03 30

www.chamonix-meteo.com

www.chamonix-weather.com

Emergency and Rescue

PGHM in Chamonix.
Tel: 50 53 16 89

PGHM St Gervais.
Tel: 04 50 78 10 81

Police Emergency France. Tel 112

Police Emergency Italy. Tel: 113

Emergency Services, Chamonix
Department. Tel: 18

*Descending towards
the Grand Mulets
from Mont Blanc*

THE CLASSIC HAUTE ROUTE

For many skiers there is only one Haute Route and this is it – the traverse between Mont Blanc and the Matterhorn. To many, even if they do not consider it the only high-level route and not even the first Alpine high-level ski route, it is the quintessential Haute Route. It is a magnificent traverse that attracts skiers from all around the world. Like many of the Alpine 'big ticks' – the Matterhorn and Mont Blanc included – its difficulty and seriousness are often underestimated. A high percentage of those who set off on the tour never complete it, and many that do seem to rely on the tracks of more skillful ski mountaineers.

To many skiers it comes as a surprise to discover that the Classic Haute Route was first called the High Level Road. It is even more of a revelation to find out that this, the most famous and coveted Alpine ski tour, came into existence as a walking route between the burgeoning Alpine centres of Chamonix and Zermatt. It should come as less of a surprise to learn that it was the 'invention' of the Alpine Club's Victorian eccentrics. By 1861 many of the club's most notable members, including Forbes,

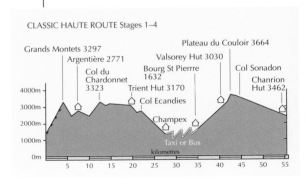

CLASSIC HAUTE ROUTE Stages 1–4

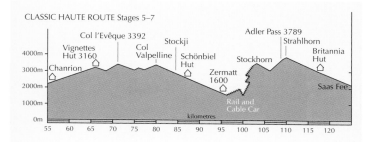

CLASSIC HAUTE ROUTE Stages 5–7

Wills, Matthews, Whymper, Tuckett, Hardy and Jacomb, had completed, more or less, a continuous traverse over the peaks, passes and glaciers between Mont Blanc and the Matterhorn.

What has become known, as the Classic Haute Route was first traversed on skis in January 1911 and included the crossing of the Plateau du Couloir – this involves some steep climbing on south side of the Grand Combin. This key section, linking the Valsorey and Chanrion Huts, is a committing undertaking, one that is avoided by the Verbier variant of the Haute Route.

Although many people describe the skiers' High Level Route as a traverse between Chamonix and Zermatt, it is really a traverse between Argentière and Zermatt. Others regard the continuation to Saas Fee, over the Adler pass, as the complete traverse. The Haute Route can be skied in either direction; however, the crossing from west to east is the most popular.

In good weather during the high season, a well-worn track can extend from Argentière to Zermatt, but it would be foolish to rely on it. In poor conditions the track soon fills in, and those unprepared or unable to navigate will definitely have problems.

Most parties starting from Argentière complete the first day to the Trient Hut by using the Grands Montets ski lift. Others opt for a more leisurely start from the Argentière Hut, which guarantees an early start and the possibility of reaching Mont Fort the same day. Others

161

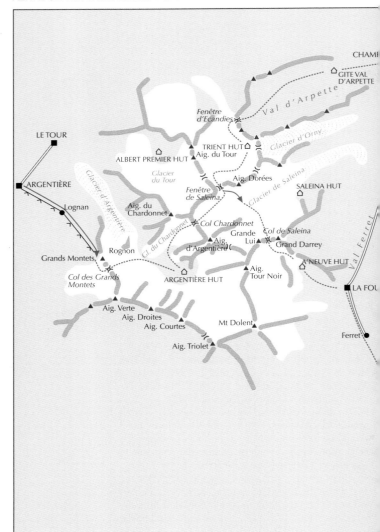

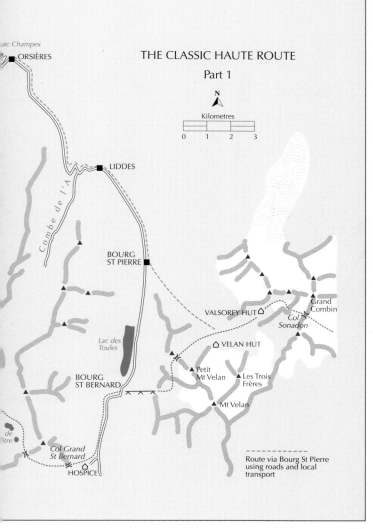

THE CLASSIC HAUTE ROUTE

Part 1

N

Kilometres

0   1   2   3

Lac Champex
ORSIÈRES

LIDDES

Combe de l'A

BOURG
ST PIERRE

VALSOREY HUT

Grand
Combin

Col
Sonadon

Lac des
Toules

☐ VELAN HUT

BOURG
ST BERNARD

▲ Petit
Mt Velan

▲ Les Trois
Frères

▲ Mt Velan

Col Grand
St Bernard

HOSPICE

- - - - - - -
Route via Bourg St Pierre
using roads and local
transport

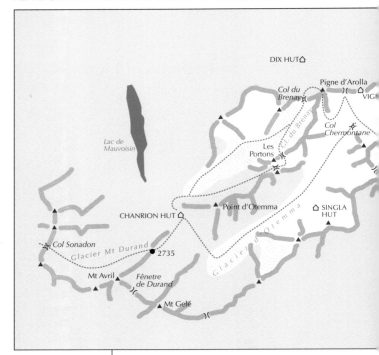

prefer a night in the Trient Hut and an early start for the Val d'Arpette, with lunch in Champex and an afternoon ride onwards. The variations are many.

By any yardstick, this is a superb tour covering some of the finest mountain terrain in the Western Alps. In its purest form, it does not climb mountains, but finds instead an adventurous way across cols and glaciers. There are many variations possible – summits can be added and variations followed that avoid the road. All are agreed, however, that the classic route should cross the Plateau du Couloir. The route described here does just that. However, I have included a couple of sought-after variations to the Classic Haute Route.

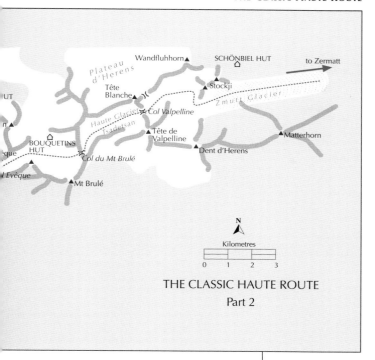

Plateau d'Hérens

Wandfluhhorn▲   SCHÖNBIEL HUT ⌂   to Zermatt

Tête
Blanche▲   ✕⤬ Col Valpelline   ▲ Stockji

▲ Tête de   *Zmutt Glacier*
Valpelline

Haute Glacier
Tsadetsan

⌂
BOUQUETINS
HUT

Col du Mt Brulé   ▲ Dent d'Herens   ▲ Matterhorn

Evêque

▲ Mt Brulé

N
▲

Kilometres

0   1   2   3

THE CLASSIC HAUTE ROUTE
Part 2

- To avoid taking road transport from Champex a continuous connection has been established over the
  Grande Lui to La Fouly in the Swiss Val Ferret. It continues via the Col du Grand St Bernard and Mont
  Velan Hut before reaching the Valsorey Hut below
  the Plateau du Couloir. In avoiding the need for road
  transport, this more difficult and interesting variation adds at least one day to the tour. This is a more
  serious undertaking and one that is less well travelled.
- The other option is to climb the Pigne d'Arolla via
  the Brenay Glacier rather than to go directly to the
  Vignettes Hut via the Otemma glacier.

The Tour

Start:	Argentière
Finish:	Zermatt or Saas Fee
Duration:	Classic Route – 7 days to Zermatt; 8 days to Saas Fee
Location:	A traverse of the Western Alps from the Mont Blanc range in France to the Matterhorn and Saas Fee in the Pennine Alps of Switzerland.
Difficulty:	BSA. PD+ – AD. A strenuous and serious tour traversing a considerable amount of steep ground as it crosses very impressive territory. Most skiers successfully complete the route only when the conditions are good and a track is in place. It is a serious and strenuous tour that should not be underestimated.
Best Time:	Mid-March to May – ideally when the huts are wardened
Facilities:	Chamonix, Argentière, Zermatt and Saas Fee are major resort centres with good road and rail links. The Haute Route is well serviced by French and Swiss mountain huts that provide a full service through the touring season. Many are overbooked during April so book in advance to ensure a reservation. The huts provide a full restaurant service and snack food is usually available. Otherwise, food for the mountain is best bought in the Chamonix valley and en route in Champex or Bourg.
Access:	Geneva Airport is less than 1 hour from Chamonix. There is a daily coach service and train service to Chamonix and Argentière. There is also an airport transfer service between the airport and valley.
Maps:	CNS: 1:50,000 Ski maps. Martigny – Sheet 282S, Arolla – Sheet 283S, Mischabel – Sheet 284S. CNS: 1:25,000 – Col du Balme Sheet 1344, Orsières – Sheet 1345, Grand St Bernard – Sheet 1344, Chanrion – Sheet 1346, Mt Vélan – Sheet 1366, Matterhorn – Sheet 1347, Zermatt – Sheet 1348, Saas – Sheet 1329. The French map IGN Chamonix 1:25,000 3630OT Top 25 is useful for the Mont Blanc end of things but the route is covered by the Swiss maps detailed.

The Aiguille d'Argentière and the Milieu glacier seen from the Col Grands Montets – on the left is the Glacier du Chardonnet, leading to Col du Chardonnet

MAIN ROUTE SUMMARY

Stage 1: Argentière, 1200m – Grands Montets, 3297m – Col des Grands Montets, 3233m – Argentière Hut, 2771m

Stage 2: Argentière Hut, 2771m – Col du Chardonnet, 3323m – Fenêtre de Saleina, 3267m – Trient Hut, 3170m

Stage 3: Trient Hut, 3170m – Champex, 1466m – Bourg St Pierre, 1632m

Stage 4: Bourg St Pierre, 1632m – Valsorey Hut, 3030m

Stage 5: Valsorey Hut, 3030m – Plateau du Couloir, 3664m – Col Sonadon – Chanrion Hut, 3462m

Stage 6: Chanrion Hut, 3462m – Otemma Glacier or Brenay Glacier – Vignettes Hut, 3160m

Stage 7: Vignettes Hut, 3160m – Col de l'Evêque, 3392m – Col Mont Brulé, 3213m – Tête de Valpelline, 3802m – Zermatt, 1600m

Stage 8: Zermatt, 1600m – Saas Fee via the Adler pass, 3789m

GRAND LUI VARIATION

This three-day variation normally leaves the Classic Haute Route at the Trient Hut and rejoins it at the Valsorey Hut (thus omitting Stages 3 and 4 of the main route). It usually adds at least an extra day to the total route. It is possible for a fast party to bypass the Trient Hut and complete the Grand Lui crossing to La Fouly in one day from the Argentière Hut. A very early start is advisable to ensure good snow conditions for the descent to La Fouly.

ROUTE SUMMARY

Stage 1: Trient Hut, 3170m – Fenêtre de Saleina, 3267m – Col de Saleina, 3419m – La Fouly, 1593m

Stage 2: La Fouly, 1593m – Fenêtre de Ferret, 2698m – Great St Bernard Hospice, 2469m

Stage 3: Great St Bernard Hospice, 2469m – Col de Prox, 2779m – Chaux de Jean Max to c.2257m – Valsorey Hut, 3030m

MAIN ROUTE ITINERARY
Stage 1

Argentière, 1200m – Grands Montets, 3297m – Col des Grands Montets, 3233m – Argentière Hut, 2771m

Ascent:	121m – if using the Grands Montets ski lift
Descent:	645m
Principal Aspect:	E
Time:	1–2 hours from Grands Montets lift station

This is the most comfortable way to begin this tour, allowing more time to acclimatise and adjust to the Alpine environment. The initial descent from Grands Montets is steep with some crevasse danger. For many skiers, as they stand on the Col des Grands Montets with a loaded rucksack and weak knees, the mixture of altitude and high-mountain ambience provides a shock to the system.

Stage 2
Argentière Hut, 2771m – Col du Chardonnet, 3323m – Fenêtre de Saleina, 3267m – Trient Hut, 3170m

Ascent:	961m
Descent:	520m
Difficulty:	A strenuous day involving steep climbing, abseiling and several changes from skiing to skinning.
Principal Aspect:	W, E, S, N
Time:	6–7hrs

From the hut, retrace your track onto the true right bank of the Argentière glacier and contour round the foot of the south-west ridge of the Aiguille d'Argentière to a point where it is possible to ascend the Glacier du Chardonnet. Depending on conditions, climb either the rocky lower slopes of the south-west ridge or steeply up the glacier right of centre ,keeping clear of the main icefall. Above the icefall at c.2800m, it is usually possible to traverse into the centre of the glacier. At this point, the climbing angle eases as the route finds a way through a zone of crevasses. Continue directly and less steeply to the Col du Chardonnet, 3323m. This is an impressive place with stunning views, if you are lucky, of the north face of the Aiguilles Verte and Droites.

From the col descend the narrow couloir on the north-east side for about 80m. The bergschrund at the foot of the couloir can usually be reached by one or more abseils and down-climbing. In good conditions, a few opt to sideslip and ski the couloir, but other descending parties may make this impossible or unsafe. From the bergschrund make a gently descending traverse NE around the Saleina glacier, passing below pt.3084. This is the foot of the rocky spur descending from the Grand Fourche. In clear weather, it should be possible to make out the narrow gap of the Fenêtre de Saleina, 3267m, at the head of the basin between the Petite Fourche, Aiguille de la Fenêtre and Aiguilles Dorées. Skin towards the notch, ascending gradually to a point more or less below it. The last 30m are steep and some-times icy, and are often best climbed on foot.

From this impressive notch traverse NE around the north spur of the Aiguilles Dorées, contouring E across

Traversing the Col Ecandies at the head of the Val d'Arpette

the Plateau du Trient heading towards the Col d'Orny, 3098m. The Trient Hut is on a rocky terrace below the Point d'Orny just above the col. Below the buttress in front of the hut and at the edge of the glacier there is normally a pronounced wind scoop, which is easy to fall into in poor visibility! This is best avoided on the left by ascending a snow slope to c.3170m before traversing right to the Trient Hut.

Stage 3

Trient Hut, 3170m – Champex, 1466m – Bourg St Pierre, 1632m

These statistics cover the route as far as Champex only.

Ascent:	50m
Descent:	1690m
Difficulty:	A magnificent descent in good conditions but hard work and disappointing in poor conditions.
Principal Aspect:	N and E
Time:	2–4 hours

This is a broken stage of the tour and in many ways unsatisfactory because road transport is normal between Champex and either Bourg St Pierre or Verbier. A few very fit or enthusiastic parties with an early start reach the Valsorey Hut the same day. However, the climb to the Valsorey is long and exposed to considerable avalanche risk after midday. Most skiers opt for a more leisurely day and spend the night in Bourg St Pierre.

It is normal to leave the Trient Hut at dawn. A delayed start may well result in difficult snow conditions in the Val d'Arpette, especially later in the season.

From the hut descend N along the true right bank of the Trient glacier to a shoulder and flat area, c.3000m. This is a point level with an icefall at the top of the Trient glacier, which is on the left and W of the Petite Pointe d'Orny. Ahead are two options to reach the upper Val d'Arpette.

The Fenêtre du Chamois: From the shoulder at c.3000m the Fenêtre du Chamois is the well-marked narrow gap in the rocky ridge S of the Col des Ecandies. Reach it by traversing NE across a steep snow slope. On the N side of the gap a steep couloir descends for 150m into the upper Val d'Arpette. Either abseil or crampon down this couloir until it is possible to ski safely to a point level with the Col des Ecandies, 2796m. This is a time-consuming descent for a large party.

The Col des Ecandies, 2796m: In good conditions, this is quite straightforward. From the shoulder, descend right of the Trient icefall keeping close to the edge of the glacier. This can be difficult in icy conditions. Descend a glacier runnel, which can be almost a couloir between the icefall on the left and the rocks on the right. It can look daunting from above and is often best descended by sideslipping. There is invariably a bergschrund to negotiate. As soon as possible, traverse north-east below the rocks of the Petite Point d'Orny to the foot of the Col des Ecandies. Ascend steeply for 50m, carrying skis, to reach the col.

From the col the narrow Val d'Arpette extends towards Champex. This can give a magnificent descent in good conditions, but the snow here changes rapidly, no doubt because of aspect and altitude. The descent can be awkward and is not without avalanche danger from the steep slopes on either side.

In the upper valley ski right of pt.2364m. The open slopes can provide enjoyable skiing. Keep more or less to the right side of the valley to reach the Relais d'Arpette, a comfortable gîte, c.1627m, and continue on a piste (it becomes a road late in the season) to the lower station of the Breya chair lift (1498m). Continue down the main street of Champex.

Many parties stop at the Refuge SAC a pleasant café/pension on the main street for a second breakfast or lunch. The bus for the onward journey stops at the post office a short distance further on. It is also possible to book a taxi at the café for the onward journey.

Those in a hurry to make the Valsorey Hut on the same day will need to make a very early start and book a taxi from the Trient Hut the night before, aiming to be met at the Relais d' Val Arpette or Breya lift station. A wiser plan for a fast team would be to traverse from the Argentière Hut to Bourg St Pierre in one day without stopping at the Trient Hut. The climb to the Valsorey Hut normally takes 5–6 hours and is best done early in the day. ▶

THE GRANDE LUI/
COL DE SALEINA VARIATION

This is a more difficult and time-consuming variation of the Haute Route, but one that will appeal to those wishing to avoid using transport between Champex and the Chanrion Hut. This magnificent variant adds at least an extra day to the total route. Most skiers opt to complete the Grande Lui variant between the Trient and Valsorey Huts in three stages. Despite being a variation, it is much more in keeping with the best stages of the 'Classic' route, and in my opinion makes the whole journey a more logical and satisfying affair. It certainly sees a lot less traffic. Good snow conditions are essential for the descent to La Fouly, but if found this section gives skiing as good, if not better, than anything else on the Haute Route. A traverse of the Col de Saleina is recommended in favour of the Col de la Grande Lui, although both are possible. Fit and acclimatised skiers leaving the Argentière Hut very early would be able to cross the Grande Lui, after crossing the Col du Chardonnet, rather than continuing to the Trient Hut. By so doing, the Grande Lui variant could then be completed in the same time as the Classic Haute Route.

Stage 1
Trient Hut, 3170m – Fenêtre de Saleina, 3267m – Col de Saleina, 3419m – La Fouly, 1593m

From the Trient Hut return across the Plateau du Trient S to the Fenêtre de Saleina, 3267m, and descend to the Glacier de Saleina at *c.*2800m.

**Champex To
Bourg St Pierre**
It is possible to take a taxi direct to Bourg St Pierre. Alternatively, there is a bus service to Orsieres (901m) in the Entremont Valley, where a second more regular service connects to Bourg St Pierre.

Ascent:	629m
Descent:	2212m
Difficulty:	BSA. PD+
Principal Aspect:	N, NE in ascent S in descent
Time:	7 hours in total

Traverse the crevassed Glacier de Saleina SE as far as a small rognon, 2887m. Now begin an ascent of the steepening glacier descending from the ridge connecting the Grande Lui and Grand Darrey. Avoid a serac band by traversing ESE close to pt.3094m before continuing more steeply S towards the Col de Saleina, 3419m. The slope leading to the col is steep and rocky near the top and is best climbed on foot. A rope may be useful here. The summit of the Grande Lui, 3509m, can be reached easily from the col by climbing a short couloir and snowed-up rocks.

From the Col de Saleina, 3419m, begin the descent of steep slopes (S3) to the S, before bearing SE (L) towards a rognon, 3040m. Skirt this to the N, below the Grand Darrey and Col de la Grande Lui, before turning S to descend superb slopes to the A'Neuve Hut, 2785m. Continue down open slopes to La Fouly. There are several hotels in La Fouly open during the season.

Stage 2
La Fouly, 1593m – Fenêtre de Ferret, 2698m – Great St Bernard Hospice, 2469m

Ascent:	1105m
Descent:	229m
Difficulty:	F
Principal Aspect:	W, N in ascent; S, E in descent
Time:	5–6 hours

Follow the road through the village up the valley to

Ferret and Les Ars Dessus and continue climbing to Plan de la Chaux. Follow the line of the summer track, crossing a steep gully, and continue ascending steep slopes to reach the most northern of the Lacs de Fenêtre, 2456m. Continue S as far as the Fenêtre de Ferret, 2698m, before making a short descent to the road at the Col du Grand St Bernard. Follow the road E to the hospice, which was founded by St Bernard of Menthon in the 10th century.

Stage 3
Great St Bernard Hospice, 2469m – Col de Prox, 2779m – Chaux de Jean Max to c.2257m – Valsorey Hut, 3030m

Ascent:	2022m without the lift
Descent:	1461m
Principal Aspect:	SW, W in ascent; NE in descent
Difficulty:	BSA. Interesting route-finding. Several S3 pitches. A long day.
Time:	9–10 hours

From the monastery, descend the road to Bourg St Bernard, 1632m. If the Les Darreys ski lift is operating, take it to pt.2273m. Begin climbing E before turning NE towards the Col de Prox, 2779m. Gain a stream-filled gully at c.2460m and climb this to c.2800m before traversing L on level ground, from where a descent leads to steeper slopes leading to the Col de Prox that are best climbed on foot.

Now begin an ascending traverse R (NE) to reach a level ridge above the small lake at 2188m. Continue on the ridge to just before Mont Orge, 2881m. Turn R and ski steeply NE down fine slopes leading to Chaux de Jean Max to c.2300m, at which point the route to the Mont Velan Hut turns R and climbs the moraine to the hut. To reach the Valsorey Hut cross the moraine and join the route from Bourg St Pierre at Grand Plans, c.2501m. Continue to pt.2614m below a rocky spur that leads directly to the Valsorey Hut.

The long climb from Bourg to the Valsorey Hut

Ahead the slopes remain steep, and there are three possible route options to reach the hut.

- Climb right (E) of the spur up a relatively uniform slope to a point where it is possible to traverse L (W) to reach the hut.
- The route shown on many ski maps climbs the slope left of the spur in a series of zigzags before reaching the hut after a rightwards (E) traverse over rocky terrain. This slope presents considerable avalanche danger in all but perfect conditions and is menaced from above by potential avalanches from the rocky slopes of Les Botseresses.
- If snow conditions seem dangerous, the most certain way to the hut is to ascend the rocky spur below the hut on foot from above pt.2614m. High on this spur, at a point marked by two cairns, traverse left before continuing more or less directly up to the hut.

MAIN ROUTE ITINERARY (CONTINUED)
Stage 4
Bourg St Pierre, 1632m – Valsorey Hut, 3030m

Ascent:	1168m
Difficulty:	A long uphill grind – best climbed in the morning. Considerable avalanche danger.
Principal Aspect:	SW and S
Time:	5–6 hours

The climb to the hut is long and unrelenting, but it is a key passage in the traverse that will be best appreciated by mountaineers who ski – a little! I think it is ambitious to include it in a traverse from the Trient Hut, but some do. Later in the day, there is invariably an increased avalanche risk.

Although the path to the Valsorey and Velan Huts is signposted, it is not always easy to find in the dark, so time in reconnaissance the night before is time well spent. From the village pass under the main road (small underpass), crossing meadows to gain the Valsorey valley, and follow this SE keeping above the true right bank (NE) of the stream. Pass the Plan du Pey, 1827m, and Cordonna huts, 1834m, and continue easily to a point below the Chalet d'Amont, 2197m. On the R there are two bridges crossing the stream. The path to the Velan Hut crosses the higher of these. The summer route to the Valsorey Hut climbs left from the Chalet d'Amont towards a rock barrier, pt.2352.5m, but this can be dangerous in winter and spring. Instead, continue more or less up the streambed as far as pt.2238m, where an obvious narrow gorge enters from the left. A large quartz-veined boulder marks its entrance.

Climb E through the gorge until you reach easier ground near the former confluence of the Tseudet and Valsorey glaciers. Follow the E lateral moraine of the Valsorey glacier before climbing NE to the Grand Plans at c.2501m. Continue to pt.2614m below a rocky spur that leads directly to the Valsorey Hut.

Ahead the slopes remain steep and there are three possible route options to reach the hut.

Traversing below the Rosa Blanche en route between the Mont Fort and Dix huts

- Climb right (E) of the spur up a relatively uniform

slope to a point where it is possible to traverse L (W) to reach the hut.

- The route shown on many ski maps climbs the slope left of the spur in a series of zigzags before reaching the hut after a rightwards (E) traverse over rocky terrain. This slope presents considerable avalanche danger in all but perfect conditions and is menaced from above by potential avalanches from the rocky slopes of Les Botseresses.

- If snow conditions seem dangerous, the most certain way to the hut is to ascend the rocky spur below the hut on foot from above pt.2614m. High on this spur, at a point marked by two cairns, traverse left before continuing more or less directly up to the hut.

Stage 5

Valsorey Hut, 3030m – Plateau du Couloir, 3664m – Col Sonadon – Chanrion Hut, 3462m

Ascent:	843m
Descent:	1411m
Difficulty:	BSA. PD. A committing day, regarded by many as the key to the Haute Route, which demands all-round ski-mountaineering skill – and good conditions. The climb to the col is steep and exposed, especially in icy conditions.
Principal Aspect:	SW and E
Time:	6–8 hours

This, the crossing of the Plateau du Couloir, Col Sonadon and Glacier Durand, is a key passage on the Classic Haute Route. It is a magnificent, albeit serious, day of ski mountaineering set amongst high peaks, passes and glaciers that should only be undertaken in good conditions – in which case the difficulties are reasonable.

This is a section of the Haute Route on which rope, axe and crampons are invariably needed. In hard snow or icy conditions, it is better to make the 600m climb to the Plateau du Couloir on foot. In soft snow it is possible to skin some way before changing to crampons, but don't leave it too late, because the change-over can be delicate and the position is exposed.

From the hut climb NE towards the Grand Combin de Valsorey over the Meitin Glacier – the first 250–300m is reasonable, and it is this section that is most often done on skis in favourable snow conditions. As the slope steepens below the Col du Meitin, slant R (ESE) to gain the Plateau du Couloir, some 150–200m left of pt.3661m. The last 100m are steep, 45–50°, and can feel exposed in icy conditions. A cornice sometimes guards the exit onto the plateau. In these circumstances, it is advisable to aim for a point where the slope merges with the rocks of the Combin de Valsorey. ◀

NB. There is an emergency bivouac shelter on the rocks of pt.3661m.

From the flat expanse of the Plateau du Couloir, below the south face of the Combin de Valsorey, descend initially SE and then more steeply ESE to the upper Sonadon glacier. Continue E less steeply and then SE to reach the Col du Sonadon, 3504m, at the foot of the south ridge of the Grand Combin de Grafeneire. Skins are sometimes needed to reach the col.

There are two options for the next section.

- From the col descend the crevassed glacier SE towards the lowest rocks of the Grand Tête de By, c.3400m. Do not attempt to descend directly down the Mont Durand Glacier because crevasses and icefalls bar the way.
- Alternatively, traverse S from the col to below pt.3526m before descending steeply to the lowest rocks of the Grand Tête de By, c.3400m, where it joins the other route.

Continue descending the true right bank of the Glacier du Mont Durand with the large icefall and crevasses well to the left. Skirt the rocks of the Tête Blanche to c.3100m before turning E and descending towards the lateral moraine and rocks on the true right (SE) bank of the glacier. Gain these between c.2800 and 2700m. Make a rising traverse across the moraine to access a terrace leading to a shoulder at pt.2735m on the long north-east ridge of Mont Avril.

From the shoulder descend SE towards the tongue of the Fenêtre Glacier before continuing NNE more steeply into the Grand Chermontane basin E of pt.2207m. This is close to a point where the Otemma stream issues from its gorge. Cross the streambed and climb NNW, passing E of the chalet at La Paume and the higher chalet of Le Neuf, to reach the Chanrion Hut some 250m further on.

The Chanrion Hut with Mont Avril beyond

Stage 6

Chanrion Hut, 3462m – Otemma Glacier or Brenay Glacier – Vignettes Hut, 3160m

There are two route options to reach the Vignettes Hut. The 'classic' and most direct route – but also the least interesting – is via the Otemma glacier. This is a long, slow haul up a flat glacier without downhill skiing, although it is possible to include the Pigne d'Arolla. It provides a semi rest day or a sure route in poor visibility. Then alternative route via the Brenay Glacier is more interesting and difficult, but a worthwhile choice in good conditions.

181

Option 1: Chanrion Hut – Otemma glacier – Col Chermontane, 3053m -Vignettes Hut

Ascent:	905m
Descent:	209m
Difficulty:	Easy. Essentially an uphill-only day, ideal in poor visibility but a bit tedious.
Principal Aspect:	SW
Time:	4–5 hours

The 'classic' and direct route goes monotonously up the Otemma glacier, a long, slow haul, albeit through fine scenery to the Col Chermotane. From the flat expanse of the col a short climb leads to the Vignettes Hut. Alas, there is no downhill to look forward to.

A few hardy souls combine this day with the traverse from the Valsorey Hut, which makes for a pretty long day.

From the Chanrion Hut retrace the route past the chalet at La Paume to gain the Grand Chermotane basin where the Otemma stream issues from its gorge. Ascend through the gorge passing the hydro dam awkwardly, but normally on the left. Continue climbing NE up the gently rising Otemma glacier towards the Petit Mont Collon, keeping slightly left of centre. The upper glacier divides around the foot of the Petit Mont Collon. At c.2950m continue N up the left branch of the Otemma glacier towards the broad Col Chermontane, 3053m. Keep to the left of the broad col aiming towards pt.3189.4m, where a short, steep slope through rocks leads to a terrace that butts against the south-east flank of the Pigne d'Arolla. Traverse N across this terrace below a small icefall on the E flank of the Pigne. The slope on the R falls away sharply. Continue the traverse, descending slightly to reach a rocky notch on the ridge that marks the Col des Vignettes. Traverse easily R (E) on the N side of this ridge to reach the Vignettes Hut and the most airily positioned outhouse in the Alps!

Option 2: Chanrion Hut – Brenay Glacier – Col du Brenay, 3639m – Pigne d'Arolla – Vignettes Hut

Skiers on the Col du Breney, with the Points du Breney behind and the Col Chermontane and the Petit Mont Collon below on the left

Ascent:	1334m
Descent:	638m
Difficulty:	PD. A route that includes a fine summit and a good descent that is more in keeping with the rest of the tour.
Principal Aspect:	SW and E
Time:	6–8 hours

This route via the Brenay glacier and the Pigne d'Arolla is highly recommended and more in keeping with the rest of the traverse. From the Chanrion make a rising traverse N and then skirt NE around the base of the Point d'Otemma in the region of pt.2624m, crossing the E lateral moraine of the Brenay glacier. Conditions will determine whether a high or low line towards the glacier is best. Continue up the true left (E) bank of the glacier, climbing E of pt.2840.1m – skirting this knoll to

Traversing steep slopes below seracs on the Pigne d'Arolla en route to the Vignettes Hut

gain the main glacier W of pt.2878m at *c*.2840m. Continue NE over easier terrain towards the confluence of the Brenay and Serpentine glaciers, aiming for a flat-tish area at the base of the rocks of La Serpentine, *c*.2900m. Continue NE up the Brenay glacier, finding a line between the rocks of La Serpentine on the left and the seracs of the glacier on the right. This is normally climbed on foot as far as the outcrop at 3300m. When conditions allow, continue more easily on skis, passing to the right of the small rocky nunatak of pt.3434m. Continue below the rocky Pointes du Brenay as far as the depression of the Col du Brenay, 3639m. From the col continue easily, climbing NE to the Pigne d'Arolla Col, 3730m, and from there a short climb N leads to the summit of the Pigne d'Arolla, 3796m, itself. On a clear day, this is a magnificent viewpoint, arguably one of the best in the Pennine Alps.

The descent to the Vignettes can be an enjoyable one, but there is considerable crevasse danger. Regain the Pigne d'Arolla Col and then descend E to *c*.3300m, level with the seracs of a small icefall on the L (N), at a

A party of two skinning roped together above the Col Serpentine en route to the Pigne d'Arolla

point where the ground ahead fall more steeply. At this point, there are two options.

- In good weather it is easy to find a point where it is possible to traverse L (NE) below the icefall and descend directly to the Pigne d'Arolla Col and the Vignettes Hut.
- In poor visibility, from c.3300m descend S towards the Col Chermotane before making a descending traverse NE at c.3200m Here a short, steep ascent, sometimes through rocks, leads to a terrace that butts against the SE flank of the Pigne d'Arolla. Traverse N across this terrace below a small icefall on the E flank of the Pigne. The slope on the R falls away sharply. Continue the traverse, descending slightly to reach a rocky notch on the ridge that marks the Col des Vignettes. Traverse easily R (E) on the N side of this ridge to reach the airily positioned Vignettes Hut.

Stage 7

Vignettes Hut, 3160m – Col de l'Evêque, 3392m –
Col Mont Brulé, 3213m – Tête de Valpelline, 3802m –
Zermatt, 1600m

Ascent:	750m
Descent:	2407m
Difficulty:	PD-. A long and magnificent day, often remembered as the highlight of the tour. Expect a wide variety of conditions.
Principal Aspect:	W, E, N and S
Time:	8–11 hours

Many regard this as the most memorable day on the Haute Route. Certainly, when the weather is clear, the panorama of peaks seen from the Tête de Valpelline, which includes the Matterhorn, Dent d'Herens, Dent Blanche, Monte Rosa and Ober Gabelhorn, has few equals. This remains a long day, crossing three cols combined with descents through impressive glacial terrain. The day's statistics are also impressive: 24km long, and over 2000m of decent involving four cols and seven glaciers. An early start is recommended if you want to find reasonable snow conditions on the descent below the Stockji to Zermatt.

From the hut regain the Col des Vignettes and retrace your route below the E flank of the Pigne d'Arolla and so gain the broad slopes of the Col Chermotane. Continue SE, passing below the north face of the Petit Mont Collon and climbing gradually in the direction of the Col de l'Evêque, 3392m. The exact line to the col will depend on the state of the crevasses.

From the Col de l'Evêque descend gently E towards pt.3263m, keeping R of a crevasse zone and aiming for the Col Collon, 3087m. From the Col Collon descend NNE down the Haute Arolla Glacier below the rocky NW face of La Vierge. Descend to c.2900m before traversing E into a glacial bowl below Mont Brulé 3585m, aiming for the Col du Mont Brulé, 3213m. In poor visibility the col can be difficult to locate and should not be mistaken for the Col de Tsa de Tsan which is further S

Outside the delightful Bouquetins Hut below Col Evêque and the Haute Arolla Glacier

Poor visibility and difficult conditions on the crossing of the Col Valpelline between Arolla and Zermatt

NB. In the case of retreat, descent can be made to the nearby Bouquetins Hut, which has a stove, fuel and blankets. It is sometimes guarded. Alternatively, a retreat to the valley and Arolla can be made via the Haute Arolla glacier.

and closer to Mont Brulé. The final 100m to the col are steep and are often best done on foot. ◀

The Col Mont Brulé marks the border between Switzerland and Italy. From it, make a descending traverse NNE into the upper basin of the Tsa de Tsan glacier, keeping left below the rocks of the Bouquetins ridge and staying well clear of an impressive icefall on the right. Begin climbing ENE towards the Col de Valpelline, 3568m, keeping to the north bank of the Tsa de Tsan glacier, below the rocks of the south face of the Tête Blanche, 3724m. The glacier steepens gradually, leading finally to the broad slopes of the Col de Valpelline. For some reason the pull to the col invariably seems longer than it should. If you are lucky and the snow conditions are good, you can look forward to a magnificent descent to Zermatt.

At this point peak-baggers may well take in either the Tête de Valpelline, 3802m, or Tête Blanche, 3724m

– both provide an outstanding balcony from which to view the surrounding peaks.

From the col, ski NE down the crevassed Stockji glacier towards the Wandflue. At c.3200m bear towards the whaleback of the Stockji, and then turn SSE before reaching it to descend a steep slope onto the Tiefmatten glacier. Avoid skiing too far R (W) on this slope, even though the angle lessens, because there is greater danger from serac fall from above. At c.2980m, turn L (NE) keeping close to the rocks of the Stockji on the true left bank of the Tiefmatten glacier. Continue descending below the Stockji until c.2600m, where the Tiefmatten and Zmutt glaciers merge.

At this point, you have a route choice.

• Cross the Zmutt glacier northwards towards the Schönbiel Hut, which is located on top of the north lateral moraine of the Zmutt glacier. In certain conditions it is possible to descend NE on the glacier below the moraine to pt.2238m, close to moraine lakes before the Stafel Hydro Scheme. Lower down, under limited snow, this route over bumpy moraine debris can be tedious.

Climbing the Tête Valpelline on a fine day with the magnificent pyramid of the Matterhorn beyond. The Zmutt ridge is the left skyline with the Italian Ridge on the right

**Continuation
to Saas Fee**
The Haute Route
route typically fin-
ishes in Zermatt, how-
ever a continuation to
Saas Fee (Stage 8) is
most worthwhile and
provides an opportu-
nity to bag the
Stralhorn, a 4000m
summit close to the
Adler pass. The cross-
ing to Saas Fee, using
uplift, can be made in
a single day from
Zermatt, although the
Britannia Hut is an
obvious stopping
point, especially for
those hoping to make
a ski ascent of the
Allalinhorn, 4027m,
followed by a magnif-
icent final run to Saas
Fee – a descent of
over 2200m.

- Alternatively, traverse to the right (S) bank of the Zmutt glacier, making a high-line, descending traverse below the north face of the Matterhorn. Beware of potential avalanche and stonefall danger from the face above. Aim for pt.2238m close to the moraine lakes before the Stafel Hydro Scheme.

At this point, both routes continue down the road of the Stafel Hydro Scheme, connecting with a marked piste (Weisse Perle) coming from Schwarzsee. The piste (walking track) leads to Furi, from where it is possible either to take the cable car to Zermatt or, if there is enough snow, to ski to Zermatt. ◀

Stage 8
Zermatt, 1600m – Adler pass, 3789m – Saas Fee

Ascent:	1170m to Strahlhorn summit
Descent:	2470m to Britannia Hut or 3800m to Sass Fee
Difficulty:	SAM. A big day to finish on. Under icy conditions, crossing the Adler feels serious, steep and exposed.
Principal Aspect:	W and E
Time:	8 hours to the Britannia Hut plus 1–2 hours to Saas Fee

There is a choice of routes to reach the Adler pass, 3789m, depending on which ski lifts are working.

If the Gornergrat railway and the cable cars to the Stockhorn are open, this is the preferred option (see below). Take the railway to the Gornergrat; this connects with a lift to the Hohtalligrat and a second lift which finishes at pt.3405m, a short distance from the Stockhorn.

Later in the season, when these lifts close, it is necessary to have an overnight stay at the Monte Rosa Hut and reach the Stockhorn pass from the hut via the Gorner glacier. Depending on conditions the Monte

Rosa hut can be reached by a descent of the Unter Theodule glacier from the Kleine Matterhorn lift, followed by an ascent of the Gorner glacier from opposite the Rifflehorn (6 hrs). Alternatively, if the train is running and snow conditions allow, the hut can be reached by a descent from the halt at Rottenboden (2hrs).

Adler Pass via the Gornergrat and Stockhorn Pass
From the cable car, walk E along the rocky spine that extends towards the Stockhorn – this can sometimes be done on skis. Pass N of the actual peak and make a descending traverse to the Stockhorn pass, 3394m, dividing the Gorner glacier from the Findel glacier. At the pass turn L (N) and descend to pt.3120m in the centre of the Findel glacier. Continue traversing NNE, crossing the glacier to reach the foot of a steep snow slope dividing the rocky south ridge of the Adlerhorn, 3988m, between pt.3421m and the Strahlchnubel, pt.3222m. Ascend this steep slope to gain the Adler glacier. Traverse N to the true right bank of the Adler glacier at 3400m, keeping below the south face of the

Traversing the Stockhorn pass en route to the Adler pass during the final stage of the Haute Route between Zermatt and Saas Fee

Rimpfischhorn. Continue climbing steeply towards the Adler pass aiming to climb it from L to R. This final slope is steep and exposed to the wind and is often icy. Although it can be climbed on skis, most parties opt for the safety of crampons and the security of a rope.

From the Adler pass, the Strahlhorn is an easy ascent. The descent returns more or less to the pass before descending NE down the true left bank of the Allalin glacier under the rockwalls of the Rimpfischhorn and the Hohlaubgrat of the Allalinhorn. At pt.3143.3 turn N to cross the Hohlaub glacier in a gently descending traverse to a point below the Hinter Allalin rock ridge where it is possible to climb a steep slope to reach the Britannia Hut, 3029m.

From the Britannia Hut a track leads NW to the Felskin ski lift and pistes that descend to Saas Fee (1–2 hrs).

On the Feejoch overlooking the Zermatt valley and the Matterhorn

THE CLASSIC HAUTE ROUTE: USEFUL INFORMATION

Huts
Argentière Hut.
Tel: 04 50 53 16 92

Trient Hut. Tel: (res) 027 722 91 58.
Tel: 027 783 14 38

Mont Fort Hut. Tel: (res) 027 771 15
91. Tel: (hut) 027 778 13 84

Velan Hut. Tel: (res) 027 785 13 13.
Tel: (hut) 027 787 13 13

Valsorey Hut. Tel: (res) 027 722 07
94. Tel: (hut) 027 787 11 22

Dix Hut. Tel: (res) 027 281 22 88.
Tel: (hut) 027 281 15 23

Chanrion Hut. Tel: (res) 027 776 13
29. Tel: (hut) 027 778 12 09

Vignettes Hut. Tel: (res) 027 283 10
34. Tel: (hut) 027 283 13 22

Schönbiel Hut. Tel: (res) 027 967 47
62 + Fax. Tel: (hut) 027 967 13 54

Monte Rosa Hut. Tel: (res) 027 967
29 08. Tel: (hut) 027 967 21 15

Britannia Hut. Tel: (res) 027 957 21
80. Tel: (hut) 027 957 22 88

Grand St Bernard Hospice.
Tel: 026 87 11 72

Useful Contacts
Grands Montets ski lift.
Tel: 50 54 00 82

Argentière Tourist Office.
Tel: 04 50 54 02 14

Chamonix Tourist Office.
Tel: 04 50 53 00 24

La Fouly Tourist Office.
Tel: 026 42 717

Zermatt Tourist Office.
Tel: 027 966 81 00

Saas Fee Tourist Office.
Tel: 027 958 1858

Park Hotel, Saas Fee.
Tel: 027 957 2426

Garni Hotel, Imseng, Saas Fee.
Tel: 027 958 1258

Weather Information
Avalanche Bulletin Haute Savoie.
Tel: 08 36 68 02 74

Chamonix Meteo.
Tel: 450 53 17 11

www.chamonix-meteo.com

Swiss Weather. Tel: 018 16 20 10

Swiss Avalanche Bulletin. Tel: 187

Six-day forecast in English
(Chamonix area).
Tel: 08 92 70 03 30

Emergency and Rescue
PGHM in Chamonix.
Tel: 50 53 16 89

PGHM St Gervais.
Tel: 04 50 78 10 81

Police Emergency France. Tel: 112

Police Emergency Italy. Tel: 113

Rega (Swiss).
Tel: 01/383 11 11/14 14

Police (Swiss). Tel: 117

Police (Italian). Tel: 113

Skier enjoying fresh powder snow above Saas Fee on the final day of the High Level Route

THE VERBIER HIGH-LEVEL ROUTE

Skiers with less time or limited mountaineering skills may prefer the Verbier variant to the Classic Haute Route. This popular alternative is less committing and avoids the big day from the Valsorey Hut over the Plateau du Couloir. It provides a more reliable route if the conditions between Bourg St Pierre and the Chanrion are unsuitable or if a party feels unsure of its technical ability to make the crossing.

It was Marcel Kurtz who first opened this variant in March 1926, as an alternative to the established route via Bourg St Pierre. Today, Verbier is a popular starting point for skiers undertaking a shortened Haute Route, but this can result in the Mont Fort, Dix and Vignettes huts being particularly crowded at weekends. It makes sense, therefore, to plan your route with this in mind, and to try to avoid the huts on these days – alternatively you will need to book your place at the huts early.

However, this is a magnificent journey in its own right and should not be underestimated – it is only slightly less difficult than the classic route, and many regard the skiing as superior. Certainly the day to the Vignettes traversing the Pigne d'Arolla from the Dix is far superior to the route up the Otemma glacier to the Vignettes.

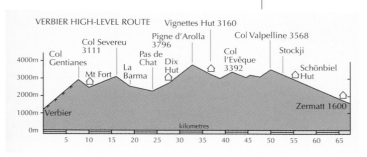

VERBIER HIGH-LEVEL ROUTE

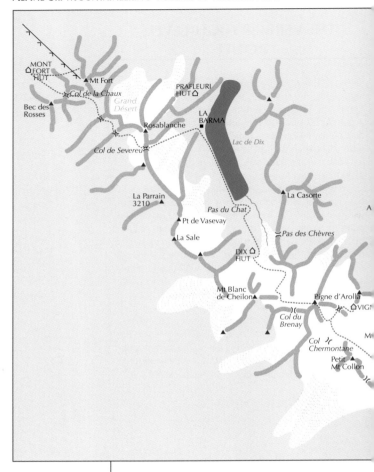

Groups wishing to start from Argentière should follow the first two stages of the Classic Haute Route as far
as Champex before continuing to Verbier by road and rail.

For parties starting at Verbier and finishing in Zermatt
this could well be called the 'Classic Short Route'. That

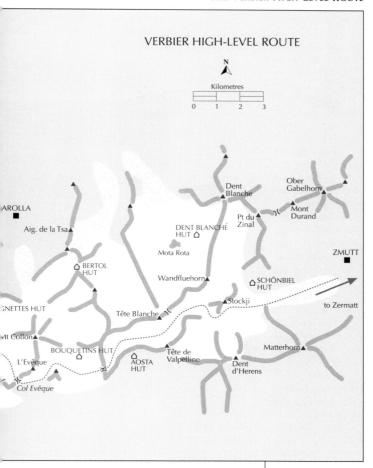

VERBIER HIGH-LEVEL ROUTE

said, it provides some really enjoyable skiing, with two particularly long days if the Prafleuri Hut is bypassed en route to the Dix.

A lot of skiers overnight at the Prafleuri Hut, thus taking two days to reach the Dix Hut from Mont Fort.

The Verbier–Zermatt traverse, done in reverse, is the course taken by the Paitrouille des Glaciers, an annual race, originally for mountain troops. It is a fantastically well-organised affair, with hundreds of teams and skiers taking part. The route is marked, and in places, on the Rosablanche, ropes are fixed in a steep couloir. This is light-weight ski randonnée at its most extreme. The competitors, best described as ski-run-ners, cover the course in an amazingly fast time (7½ hours). The race usually takes place in May, which is certainly the time to avoid this tour. However, in the week prior to the race small flags are stuck in the snow to mark the route over the Rosablanche, and many skiers have found these useful in poor visibility!

This has the advantage of allowing the traverse along the Dix reservoir, which can present considerable avalanche danger, to be completed early in the day. ◀

Retreat to the Arolla valley for rest and recuperation (beer and bread) during bad weather on the Haute Route

The Tour

ROUTE SUMMARY

Stage 1: Mt Fort Hut. Getting to the Mt Fort Hut can hardly be called a stage, since it's really only a matter of descending from the Mt Fort lift to the hut. However, it is essential to be in position at the hut, as this allows an early start for the Dix Hut on what is a long day.

Stage 2: To the Dix Hut via Three Cols

Stage 3: Dix Hut to Vignettes Hut via the Pigne d'Arolla

Stage 4: Vignettes Hut – Col de l'Evêque – Col Mont Brulé

Start:	Verbier
Finish:	Zermatt or Saas Fee
Duration:	4–5 days
Location:	The route lies wholly within the canton Valais in SW Switzerland and traverses the peaks of the Western Pennine Alps south of the Swiss Rhone valley.
Difficulty:	SAM. PD.
Best Time:	Mid-March to mid-May
Facilities:	Verbier is a major ski station with a wide range of accommodation, including an inexpensive dortoir at the sport centre. Equipment stores and supermarkets.
Access:	Geneva is the nearest international airport. There is a fast rail service between Geneva and Martigny, and an onward connection to Les Chable. A cable car or bus service connects it to Verbier.
Maps:	CNS: 1:50,000 Ski maps. Martigny – Sheet 282S, Arolla – Sheet 283S, Mischabel – Sheet 284S. CNS: 1:25,000 –Rosablanche – Sheet 1326, Chanrion – Sheet 1346, Matterhorn – Sheet 1347, Zermatt – Sheet 1348, Saas – Sheet 1329

– Tête de Valpelline – Zermatt
Stage 5: Zermatt – the Adler pass – Saas Fee

ROUTE ITINERARY
Stage 1
Mt Fort Hut – Three Cols – Dix Hut

Ascent:	1225m
Descent:	725m
Difficulty:	PD. Short pitches of S3 below Col de la Rionde and Col de Severeu. A long day out, with complex route-finding over the three cols, followed by a long, flat section alongside the Lac Dix. The traverse alongside the Dix reservoir presents a known avalanche risk.
Principal Aspect:	SW and E
Time:	8–10 hours

From the hut climb SE, crossing moraines to reach the diminishing Chaux glacier. Ascend ESE to the Col de la Chaux, 2940m. Descend SE into a small lake basin (2764m) below the SW flank of Petit Mont Fort. Pass this on the L. Now climb SE towards the Col de Momin. Before reaching the col traverse R (SE) below rocks to reach a small col at pt.3039m (Col de la Rionde). Descend a steep, broad gully on the far side and re-ascend SE to reach the Col de Severeu, 3111m. From the col descend steeply E to reach the lateral moraine of the Ecoulaies glacier. Continue descending ENE over broad and open slopes towards the Barma huts. From just above the huts begin a traverse SSE above the Dix Lake to pt.2386m before the Pas du Chat. It is usual to employ a bit of poling on this often tedious section. This is a known avalanche slope.

Cross the stream and climb E below rocky slopes. Continue climbing SE to pt.2581m, following a small valley SSE to below the Tête Noire. A short descent leads to the true left bank of the Cheilon glacier. Pass under the hut and make an ascending traverse to the top of the moraine and turn sharply R to the Dix Hut.

Traversing the Col de Severeu, 3192m, on the flanks of the Rosablanche overlooking the Dix valley

Stage 2

Dix Hut – Pigne d'Arolla – Vignettes Hut

Ascent:	868m
Descent:	636m
Difficulty:	PD. The Col Serpentine is steep and exposed in icy conditions.
Principal Aspect:	NW, N and E
Time:	5–6 hours

This stage presents a magnificent ski-mountaineering day, and is one of the best stages on the Haute Route, classic or otherwise.

From the hut descend steeply SE onto the Cheilon glacier before putting on skins. Ascend SE across the broad slopes of the Cheilon glacier towards pt.3029m to gain the broad glacier bay below the Points de Tsena Refien. Ascend at first E and then NE, following a ramp into the bay, which can be badly crevassed. Turn SE and begin climbing more steeply to reach pt.3423m, above the icefall, where the slope eases. Continue SW along a broad spur leading towards the Col de la Serpentine. At c.3500m bear L (SE), traversing the open slopes of the upper basin of the Tsidjiore Nouve to gain the foot of the Mur de la Serpentine. Climb steeply up the Mur de la Serpentine to pt 3592m. In icy conditions this exposed slope is often best climbed on foot. At the top of this slope, the angle eases and opens into a glacier bowl. Continue climbing gently SE towards the Col du Breney, 3639m. From below the col continue easily NE to the Col Pigne d'Arolla, 3730m, from where a short climb N leads to the summit of the Pigne d'Arolla, 3796m, itself. On a clear day this is a magnificent viewpoint – arguably one of the best in the Pennine Alps.

The descent to the Vignettes, in good conditions, can be an enjoyable one, but there is considerable crevasse danger. The slope also gets the sun throughout the morning. Regain the Pigne d'Arolla Col and descend E to c3300m, a point level with the seracs of a small icefall on the L (N), where the ground falls away sharply. At this point there are two options.

- In good weather it is easy to find the place where it is possible to traverse L (NE) underneath the icefall and descend directly to the Col des Vignettes on the rocky ridge leading to the Vignettes Hut. Cross the ridge and traverse to the hut.

- In poor visibility, from c.3300m descend S towards the Col Chermotane before making a descending traverse NE at c.3200m. Here a short, steep ascent, sometimes through rocks, leads to a terrace that butts against the SE flank of the Pigne d'Arolla. Traverse N across this terrace below a small icefall on the E flank of the Pigne. The slope on the R falls away sharply. Continue the traverse, descending slightly to reach a rocky notch on the ridge that marks the Col des Vignettes. Traverse easily R (E) on the N side of this ridge to reach the airily positioned Vignettes Hut.

Stage 3
Vignettes Hut – Col de l'Evêque – Col Mont Brulé – Tête de Valpelline – Zermatt

Ascent:	750m
Descent:	2407m
Difficulty:	PD-. A long day with several climbs over serious glacier terrain.
Principal Aspect:	W, E, N and S
Time:	8–10 hours

A long and magnificent day, one that many regard as the highlight of the tour. Certainly, when the weather is clear, the panorama of peaks seen from the Tête de Valpelline, which includes the Matterhorn, Dent d'Herens, Dent Blanche, Monte Rosa and Ober Gabelhorn, has few equals. This remains a long day, crossing three cols combined with descents through impressive glacial terrain. The day's statistics are also

impressive: 24km long, and over 2000m of descent involving four cols and seven glaciers. It goes without saying that an early start is recommended if you want to find reasonable snow conditions on the descent below the Stockji to Zermatt.

From the hut regain the Col des Vignettes and retrace your route below the E flank of the Pigne d'Arolla and so gain the broad slopes of the Col de Chermotane. Continue SE, passing below the north face of the Petit Mont Collon and make a long ascent to the Col de l'Evêque, 3392m. The exact line to the col will depend on the state of the crevasses.

From the Col de l'Evêque descend gently E towards pt.3263m, keeping R of a crevasse zone and aiming for the Col Collon, 3087m. From the Col Collon descend NNE down the Haute Arolla glacier below the rocky NW face of La Vierge. Descend to c.2900m before traversing E into a glacial bowl beneath Mont Brulé, 3585m, aiming for the steep slope below the Col du Mont Brulé, 3213m. In poor visibility the col can be difficult to locate and should not be mistaken for the Col de Tsa de Tsan, which is further S and closer to Mont

Below the north flank of Mont Blanc de Cheilon en route to the Col Serpentine

NB. In the case of retreat descent can be made to the nearby Bouquetins Hut, which has a stove, fuel and blankets. It is sometimes guarded. Alternatively, a retreat to the valley and Arolla can be made via the Haute Arolla glacier.

Brulé. The final 100m to the col are steep and are often best done on foot. ◀

The Col Mont Brulé marks the border between Switzerland and Italy. From it, make a descending traverse NNE into the upper basin of the Tsa de Tsan glacier, keeping left below the rocks of the Bouquetins Ridge and staying well clear of an impressive icefall to the right. Begin climbing ENE towards the Col de Valpelline, 3568m, keeping to the north bank of the Tsa de Tsan glacier, below the rocks of the south face of the Tête Blanche, 3724m. The glacier steepens gradually, leading finally to the broad slopes of the Col de Valpelline. For some reason the pull to the col invariably seems longer than it should. If you are lucky and the snow conditions are good you can look forward to a magnificent descent to Zermatt.

At this point peak-baggers may well take in either the Tête de Valpelline, 3802m, or Tête Blanche, 3724m – both provide an outstanding balcony from which to view the surrounding peaks.

The descent ventures NE from the col initially, following the highly crevassed Stockji glacier towards the Wandflue. At c.3200m it turns towards the whaleback of the Stockji, but bears SSE just before it to descend a steep slope onto the Tiefmatten glacier. Avoid skiing too far R (W) on this slope, even though the angle lessens, because there is danger from serac fall. At c.2980m turn L (NE), keeping close to the rocks of the Stockji on the true left bank of the Tiefmatten glacier. Continue descending below the Stockji until c.2600m, where the Tiefmatten and Zmutt glaciers merge.

At this point you have a route choice.
- Cross the Zmutt glacier northwards towards the Schönbiel Hut, which is located on top the north lateral moraine of the Zmutt glacier. In certain conditions it is possible to descend NE on the glacier below the moraine to pt.2238m, close to moraine lakes, before the Stafel Hydro Scheme. Lower down, under limited snow, this route over bumpy moraine debris can be tedious.

- Alternarively, traverse to the right (S) bank of the Zmutt glacier, maintaining a high-line on a descending traverse below the north face of the Matterhorn. Beware of avalanche and stonefall danger from the glacier above. Aim for pt.2238m, close to the moraine lakes before the Stafel Hydro Scheme. Later in the season this is often the end of the skiable snow – in which case shoulder skis and continue on foot to Furi or Zermatt.

At this point both routes continue down the road of the Stafel Hydro Scheme, connecting with a marked piste (Weisse Perle) coming from Schwarzsee. The piste (walking track) leads to Furi, from where it is possible either to take the cable car to Zermatt, or if there is enough snow, to ski to Zermatt. ▶

Stage 4
Zermatt – Adler pass – Saas Fee

Ascent:	1170m to Strahlhorn summit
Descent:	2470m to Britannia Hut or 3800m to Sass Fee
Principal Aspect:	W and E
Time:	8 hours to the Britannia hut, plus 1–2 hours to Saas Fee
Difficulty:	A big day to finish on. Under icy conditions crossing the Adler feels serious and exposed.

There is a choice of routes to reach the Adler pass, 2789m, depending on which ski lifts are working.

If the Gornergrat railway and the cable cars to the Stockhorn are open, this is the preferred option. Take the railway to the Gornergrat, this connects with a lift to the Hohtalligrat and a second lift which finishes at pt.3405m, a short distance from the Stockhorn.

Later in the season, when these lifts close, it is necessary to have an overnight stay at the Monte Rosa Hut

Continuation to Saas Fee
The Haute Route route typically finishes in Zermatt. However, a continuation to Saas Fee is most worthwhile and provides an opportunity to bag the Stralhorn, a 4000m summit close to the Adler pass. The crossing to Saas Fee, using uplift, can be made in a single day from Zermatt, although the Britannia Hut is an obvious stopping point, especially for those hoping to make a ski ascent of the Allalinhorn, 4027m, followed by a magnificent final run to Saas Fee – a descent of over 2200m.

At the top of the steep section on the climb from the Col Serpentine to the Col du Brenay en route to the Pigne d'Arolla

and reach the Stockhorn pass from the hut via the Gorner glacier. Depending on conditions the Monte Rosa Hut can be reached by a descent of the Unter Theodule glacier from the Kleine Matterhorn lift followed by an ascent of the Gorner glacier from opposite the Rifflehorn (6 hrs). Alternatively, if the train is running, and snow conditions allow, the hut can be reached by a descent from the halt at Rottenboden (2hrs).

To reach the Adler pass from the Gornergrat take the cable cars to the Stockhorn. From the cable car, walk E along the rocky spine that extends towards the Stockhorn – this can sometimes be done on skis. Pass N of the actual peak and make a descending traverse to the Stockhorn pass, 3394m, dividing the Gorner glacier from the Findel glacier.

At the pass turn L (N) and descend to pt.3120m in the centre of the Findel glacier. Continue traversing NNE, crossing the glacier to reach the foot of a steep snow slope dividing the rocky south ridge of the Adlerhorn, 3988m, between pt.3421m and the Strahlchnubel, pt.3222m. Ascend this steep slope to gain the Adler glacier. Traverse N to the true right bank of the Adler glacier at 3400m, keeping below the south face of the Rimpfischhorn. Continue climbing steeply towards the Adler pass, aiming to climb it from L to R. This final slope is steep and exposed to the wind and is often icy. Although it can be climbed on skis most parties opt for the safety of crampons and the security of a rope.

From the Adler pass the Strahlhorn is an easy ascent. The descent returns more or less to the pass before descending NE down the true left bank of the Allalin glacier under the rockwalls of the Rimpfischhorn and the Hohlaubgrat of the Allalinhorn. At pt.3143.3 turn N to cross the Hohlaub glacier in a gently descending traverse to a point below the Hinter Allalin rock ridge, where it is possible to climb a steep slope to reach the Britannia Hut, 3029m.

From the Britannia Hut a track leads NW to the Felskin ski lift and pistes that lead to Saas Fee (1–2 hrs).

Leaving the Vignettes Hut on the final leg of the High Level Route to Zermatt

VERBIER HAUTE ROUTE: USEFUL INFORMATION

Huts
Huts in general are guarded from
the end of March until the end of
May. However, this does vary a little, and you should always contact
the hut to find out and make your
booking.

Mont Fort Hut.
Tel (hut): 027 778 13 84.
Tel (res): 027 771 15 91

Dix Hut.
Tel (hut): 027 281 15 223.
Tel (res): 027 281 22 88

Vignettes Hut.
Tel (hut): 027 283 13 22.
Tel (res): 027 283 10 34

Schönbiel Hut.
Tel (hut): 027 967 13 54.
Tel (res): 027 967 47 62 + Fax

Monte Rosa Hut.
Tel (hut): 027 967 21 15.
Tel (res): 027 967 29 08

Britannia Hut.
Tel (hut): 027 957 22 88.
Tel (res): 027 957 21 80

Useful Contacts
Verbier Tourist Office.
Tel: 026/31 35 85

Zermatt Tourist Office.
Tel: 027 966 81 00

Saas Fee Tourist Office.
Tel: 027 958 18 58

Park Hotel, Saas Fee.
Tel: 027 957 24 46

Garni Hotel, Imseng.
Tel 027 957 24 46

Dortoirs in Verbier
Verbier Backpackers 'The
Bunker'. Tel: 027 771 66 02

Abri Centre Sportif.
Tel: 027 771 66 01

Emergency and Rescue
Rega (Swiss).
Tel: 01/383 11 11/14 14

Police (Swiss). Tel: 117

Police (Italian). Tel: 113

AROLLA HIGH-LEVEL CIRCUIT

When the weather turns nasty and retreat to the valley seems the only sensible option, Arolla has often become the bolt hole for skiers en route between Chamonix and Zermatt. Easily reached from the Dix, Vignettes and Bouquetins huts, the village also serves as the ideal starting point for a number of fine hut-to-hut tours. This, in my experience, is the best high-level circuit of the Arolla region, with a delightful detour into a remote corner of the Valpelline.

Arolla seems to resist change and remains very much as it was in the earliest days of Alpinism. This was a time when members of the Alpine Club stayed at the Hotel Mont Collon, enjoying its fine dining room and magnificent views. I'm certain, even now, that their ghosts would have little trouble finding their favourite

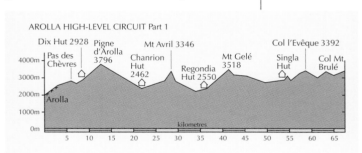

AROLLA HIGH-LEVEL CIRCUIT Part 1

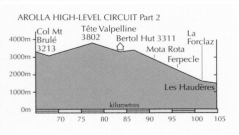

AROLLA HIGH-LEVEL CIRCUIT Part 2

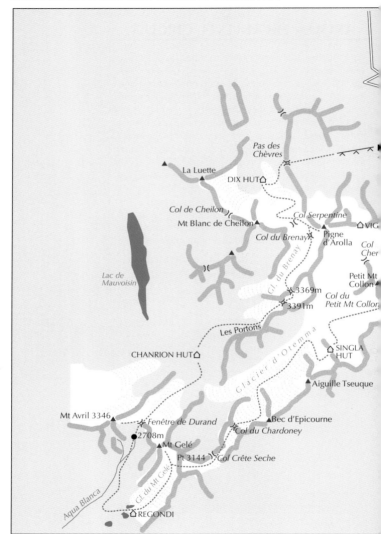

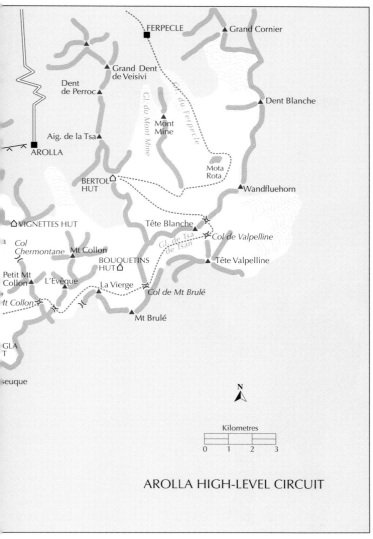

FERPECLE

▲ Grand Cornier

▲

▲ Grand Dent
de Veisivi

Dent
de Perroc ▲

Gl. du Mont Mine

Gl. du Ferpecle

▲ Dent Blanche

Aig. de la Tsa ▲

■
AROLLA

▲
Mont
Mine

BERTOL ⌂
HUT

Mota
Rota

▲ Wandfluehorn

⌂ VIGNETTES HUT

Tête Blanche ▲

Col de Valpelline

a
Col
Chermontane   Mt Collon
▲

Gl. de Tsa
de Tsan

BOUQUETINS
HUT ⌂

▲ Tête Valpelline

Petit Mt
Collon ▲   L'Evêque
▲

La Vierge
▲

Col de Mt Brulé

Mt Collon

Mt Brulé

GLA
T

seuque

N

Kilometres

0   1   2   3

AROLLA HIGH-LEVEL CIRCUIT

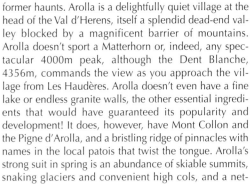

Traversing avalanche debris above Arolla at the start of the High Level Circuit, with Mont Collon and the Haute Arolla glacier beyond

former haunts. Arolla is a delightfully quiet village at the head of the Val d'Herens, itself a splendid dead-end valley blocked by a magnificent barrier of mountains. Arolla doesn't sport a Matterhorn or, indeed, any spectacular 4000m peak, although the Dent Blanche, 4356m, commands the view as you approach the village from Les Haudères. Arolla doesn't even have a fine lake or endless granite walls, the other essential ingredients that would have guaranteed its popularity and development! It does, however, have Mont Collon and the Pigne d'Arolla, and a bristling ridge of pinnacles with names in the local patois that twist the tongue. Arolla's strong suit in spring is an abundance of skiable summits, snaking glaciers and convenient high cols, and a network of comfortable huts. These all add up to perfect ski-touring terrain that can be used to meet the needs of novice and expert alike.

Despite being tiny the village offers a suprising variety of comfortable accommodation, from dortoirs to hotels. It also boasts a sports store, post office, cafés, general store and supermarket – in fact, everything you need as a base for touring. It also has a simple lift system which gives access to some quiet and enjoyable skiing, both on- and off-piste, which is ideal for a shake-down before beginning a tour.

The touring options around Arolla are abundant, and several huts provide an ideal base from which to bag numerous summits. This tour, although a hut-to-hut traverse, is not a linear one, but a high-level, almost circular tour of the peaks, passes and glaciers surrounding Arolla itself. As well as covering a short section of the popular Haute Route it visits some less frequented corners of the Haute Valais. The route just about turns full circle when it ends in Les Haudères a few kilometres down the valley. Either village would be a good base from which to start the tour, as they are both connected by a regular post-bus service.

Even during the main touring season two of the huts used on this tour are unguarded, which means you will have to be self-sufficient and carry food for those stages. They are comfortable huts, but I recommend that you carry a gaz stove and fuel. Their position and ambience easily compensate for the extra effort of carrying and cooking.

The Tour

Start:	Arolla
Finish:	Les Haudères. You have to pass through this tiny village en route to Arolla. Regular post-bus connection.
Duration:	6 days
Location:	In the western half of the Pennine Alps nestling between the Grand Combine and the Matterhorn.
Difficulty:	BSA. Ascents are mainly PD. There are some long days with a considerable amount of ascent and descent. The final descent to Les Haudères is the most difficult section of the tour, is graded AD and should only be undertaken in good conditions. It can be avoided. Serious glacier terrain exists throughout the tour and there are a number of short, steep S3 pitches.
Huts:	At least two of the huts are small, unguarded bivouac huts, therefore food and a stove will have to be carried for Stages 3 and 4. The huts are comfortable and have blankets and a selection of utensils. One has a stove, but don't rely on a

supply of gaz. It may be possible to purchase some food supplies at the Chanrion Hut, but it is worth phoning the guardian to find out. The wardened huts are normally guarded from the end of March until the end of May. Because they are on the Haute Route advanced booking is essential. All huts have a winter room, stove and fuel.

Best Time: Mid-March to May

Facilities: Arolla and Les Haudères are both convenient starting points for the tour. Both offer a variety of accommodation, and have cafés, sports stores and small supermarkets. Limited resupply may be possible at the wardened huts.

Access: Geneva is the nearest airport. Zurich is also convenient. There is a rail connection to Sion in the Rhône valley and a regular post-bus from the station to Arolla via Evolene and Les Haudères. Arolla is accessible by road, which is open year round.

Equipment: Stove and fuel recommended for the bivouac huts

Maps: Landeskarte Der Schweiz 1:50,000 series in two sheets: Arolla 283S (with ski routes marked), and Valpelline 293. Landeskarte Der Schweiz 1:25,000 series in three sheets: Evolene 1327, Chanrion 1346, Matterhorn 1347.

ROUTE SUMMARY

Stage 1: Arolla, 1998m –Pas des Chèvres, 2855m– La Luette, 3548m– Dix Hut, 2928m

Stage 2: Dix Hut, 2928m – Pigne d'Arolla, 3796m – Brenay Glacier – Les Portons – Chanrion Hut, 2462m

Stage 3: Chanrion Hut, 2462m – Mt Avril, 3346m – Regondi Bivouac Hut, 2550m

Stage 4: Regondi Bivouac Hut, 2550m – Mont Gelé, 3518m – Bivouac de l'Aiguillette (Singla), 3198m

Stage 5: Bivouac de l'Aiguillette, 3198m – Col du Petit Mt Collon, 3292m – Col de l'Evêque, 3392m – Col du Mt Brulé, 3213m – Col du Valpelline, 3568m – Col de la Tête Blanche, 3600m – Bertol Hut, 3311m

Stage 6: Bertol Hut, 3311m – Tête Blanche, 3724m – Wandflue, 3589m– Mota Rota, 3253m– Glacier Ferpecle – Les Haudères, 1452m

ROUTE ITINERARY
Stage 1
Arolla, 1998m –Pas des Chèvres, 2855m – La Luette, 3548m – Dix Hut, 2928m

Ascent:	900m to the hut, plus 440m to La Luette summit
Descent:	100m, plus 440m
Difficulty:	SAM. F. A gentle traverse to the hut. Descent of the vertical ladders from the Pas des Chèvres offers the greatest challenge.
Principal Aspect:	E
Time:	3 hours to the hut plus 2 hours for La Luette

Looking S towards (L to R) Pigne d'Arolla, Pointes de Tsena Refien and Mont Blanc de Cheilon from Mont Dolin, above Arolla

Take the Fontanettes I ski lift, which starts just above the last hairpin bend on the road leading to the village. It is not necessary to transfer to the upper tow. If the lift is closed climb the lower slopes to the end of the first tow, c.2500m. From there climb gently W, passing under the

**Ascent of La
Luette, 3548m**

If snow conditions
remain firm and you
arrive early at the hut,
an ascent of this peak is
a excellent option and
can easily be under-
taken in about 2 hours.
Descend SW from
the hut, in the direction
of the Col de Cheilon,
before turning W to
climb into the basin of
the Glacier de la
Luette. Cross a band of
moraine bearing SW in
the direction of
pt.3172.4m. Continue
in the direction of a
small col well seen on
the south-east ridge of
La Luette between the
summit and pt.3444m.
From the col it is
sometimes possible to
continue to the summit
on skis. Alternatively,
make a depot at the col
and ascend the final
ridge on foot. The
slopes leading back to
the hut are wide, offer-
ing a choice of
descents. It is worth
spying out a good line
on the way up.
Otherwise descend by
your route of ascent.

*Descending the ladders
of the Pas de Chèvres
en route to the Dix Hut*

second tow towards the Pas des Chèvres. The valley
steepens and narrows, and is best ascended on the L as
you gain height. The track may well cross several avalanche cones! The final ascent to the Pas des Chèvres,
2855m, is quite steep. From the col descend the far side
by vertical ladders – 30m. From the base of the ladders
make a diagonal descent SW across steep snow slopes
to gain the Glacier de Cheilon. Continue across the glacier SW in the direction of the hut, which can be seen
high above the far bank on a rocky outcrop near the Tête
Noir. From a point below the hut make a diagonal ascent
of the moraine to the S to gain its crest before turning N
to reach the hut. ◀

Stage 2
Dix Hut, 2928m – Pigne d'Arolla, 3796m – Brenay Glacier
– Les Portons – Chanrion Hut, 2462m

From the hut regain the Glacier de Cheilon by a steep
descent of the moraine, which in the early hours of the
morning and in the dark can be amusing. It can also be
quite crowded, especially at the weekend, as the first
part of the day forms part of the Verbier Variant of the
Haute Route. Don't despair, as it is also one of the most
scenic and enjoyable parts of that tour.

Ascent:	950m
Descent:	1335m
Difficulty:	PD. Col Serpentine S3. Exposed when icy.
Principal Aspect:	N in ascent; SW in descent
Time:	5–6 hours

Now begins the climb. Make a slow traverse of the glacier going SSE to gain the impressive cirque below the Pointes de Tsena Reifen. Go towards the obvious ice cliff and seracs before making a broad sweep NE to ascend a ramp below the icefall. Follow this until it is possible to turn back E and then S, skirting below the Pointes de Tsena Reifen and climbing steeply for a while to gain a more gentle plateau above the ice cliffs – c.3400m. Continue SW towards the Col de la Serpentine. The view to the E opens out at this point, silhouetting the distinctive Dent Blanche.

From the Col Serpentine the way ahead is barred by a cliff of snow and ice. To the left the angle relents – this

Ascending the Tsena Refien Glacier below the Col Serpentine

Looking towards the Pigne d'Arolla, 3796m, and Col du Brenay from near the Col Serpentine

is the Mur de la Serpentine. Make a ascending traverse of this slope, which is exposed in places and can be difficult in icy conditions. As you traverse L the exposure is considerable, and the slope is prone to windslab. In some conditions it is better to carry skis up this slope to reach a flat area, c.3600m, which gives access to the Col du Brenay, 3639m. The summit of the Pigne d'Arolla is not far away.

At this point there is a large glacier bowl ahead. Traverse it in a circular sweep to the SE, ascending slowly E towards a small saddle on the ridge S of the Pigne d'Arolla. Bear L of the saddle and climb easily N to reach the summit, pt.3796m. Without doubt this is the finest viewpoint in the area. In good conditions the Alps are spread around you in a great semi-circle from Mont Blanc to the Matterhorn.

From the summit, return to the Col du Brenay, 3639m. Cross this to the S and descend the crevassed Glacier du Brenay SE initially and then SSW. Descend to c.3400m before crossing towards the true left (E) bank of the glacier to gain a snow saddle, W of and below pt.3471m, on the Pointes du Brenay. This leads to a more abrupt col, the North Col du Portons, 3369m. Descend this steeply, and as soon as possible contour SW around a snowy basin before making a short ascent to yet another small col, 3391m. Cross this and descend the marvellous slopes of Les Portons to the SW. Continue a diagonal descent across the north flank of the Pointe d'Otemma, descending towards pt.2624m. Continue W to pt.2522m before turning due S to reach the Chanrion Hut, 2462m, at the end of a marvellous traverse.

Stage 3
Chanrion Hut, 2462m – Mt Avril, 3346m – Regondi Bivouac Hut, 2550m

Much of the through traffic at the Chanrion will be leaving early en route to the Vignettes. This route takes you to the Fenêtre de Durand, 2797m. The summit of Mont Avril, marking the Swiss/Italian frontier, offers a superb

Ascent:	1336m (includes Mt Avril)
Descent:	1248m (includes Mt Avril)
Difficulty:	SAM. PD
Principal Aspect:	E and NW in ascent; E and W in descent
Time:	Mt Avril 4–5 hours in ascent. 6–7 hours in total.

balcony from which to view the Grand Combin, Mont Gelé and the more distant Mont Blanc.

From the hut make a diagonal descent S to the Otemma stream, *c.*2260m. Cross the stream and climb to the SW to gain the foot slopes descending from the Fenêtre de Durand, 2797m. Climb these towards the col, but at *c.*2700m begin a rising traverse to the R to gain the snowy east flank of Mont Avril. Climb as high as possible towards the summit before making a ski depot and climbing the sloping summit rocks on foot.

Return to the ski depot and descend the slopes of the east flank, making a traverse to the Fenêtre de Durand. It is obviously possible to bypass the peak and cross the Fenêtre de Durand and continue directly to the hut.

On the far side of the col descend SW, pass N of a small lake, 2708m, probably hidden under snow, to ski steepening slopes into the drainage system of the Aqua Bianca stream descending to pt.2378m. Bear S to reach the main valley floor, which is crossed to the S. Descend SW, toward the Piano di Breuil for *c.*300m, before climbing the side of the valley to the S. At this point it is possible to reach an obvious terrace close to the small lake dell' Incliousa, 2420m. From the lake ascend NE to the colourful but small Regondi Bivouac (six places), situated between the tiny lakes of di Leitoux, 2538m, and Beuseya, 2513m. This a great place to spend the night. The hut is in a brilliant location, one that feels suprisingly remote considering that it is a relatively short descent to Ollomont and Valpelline. It provides a perfect starting point for the following day's ascent of Mont Gelé.

*Descending the
Brenay Glacier en
route to the Col
Portons and the
Chanrion Hut*

Stage 4
Regondi Bivouac Hut, 2550m – Mont Gelé 3518m –
Bivouac de l'Aiguillette (Singla), 3198m

Ascent:	1784m
Descent:	1159m
Difficulty:	SAM. A long day through some well-crevassed terrain. Difficult in poor visibility.
Principal Aspect:	S, SWS and NW in ascent; S, E and N in descent
Time:	7–8 hours

Approaching the Singla Hut in poor visibility

A fine ascent and traverse of a splendid peak in a remote Alpine backwater. Leave the hut and make a slanting ascent to the E to gain an obvious sloping ice shelf, below Mont Morion, on the Glacier du Mont Gelé. Follow this terrace easily NNE, climbing towards Mont Gelé. At *c*.3150m the glacier steepens and narrows before widening to form the south face of Mont Gelé. Ascend this, finding a way through a crevasse zone, to a high point E of the summit. From a ski depot, gain the summit ridge and follow its narrow crest to the summit.

Descend by the route of ascent passing through the narrows, bearing L to a small col on the ridge, pt.3144m. Cross this and descend steeply on the E side into the Combe de Crête Seche before bearing L to begin contouring towards the Col de Crête Seche, 2899m.

Instead of crossing the col, bear R following a narrow glacial hollow to the well-situated Col du Chardoney, 3185m. On its far side is the bowl of the delightful Glacier d'Epicourne, which hangs high above the snout of the Otemma glacier. Contour around the head of the bowl, until arriving under pt.3092m. From here turn N and descend towards the base of the south ridge of the Pointes du Jardin des Chamois. Leave the glacier at this point, bearing R to descend the steep slopes of the Jardin des Chamois and so reach the Glacier d'Otemma. With care it is possible to slant NE on the descent to reach the Otemma glacier and thereby save a bit of climbing.

Skin up the true left bank of the Otemma glacier, skirting below pt.2971m at the toe of the north ridge of the Aouille Tseuque, 3554m. On the R is a glacier bay and a small icefall. Climb steeply E, finding a way through crevasses to a more level area at *c.*3150m. At this point it is possible to traverse N to the delightfully

Descending to the Chanrion Hut

situated Bivouac de l'Aiguillette (or Singla Bivouac), 3198m, on the rocky north-west ridge of the Bec de la Sasse. The hut is comfortable and well equiped. When I last stayed it had dry blankets, a gaz stove, cooking utensils and a large amount of Swiss army rations.

Stage 5

Bivouac de l'Aiguillette, 3198m – Col du Petit Mt Collon, 3292m – Col de l'Evêque, 3392m – Col du Mt Brulé, 3213m – Col du Valpelline, 3568m – Col de la Tête Blanche, 3600m – Bertol Hut, 3311m

Ascent:	1100m
Descent:	1000m
Difficulty:	F. Some steep climbing to the cols, but the main difficulties relate to crevasses and route-finding.
Principal Aspect:	W in ascent; E in descent
Time:	6–8 hours

A magnificent traverse covering a lot of country – several cols are crossed and glaciers climbed, all amid spectacular scenery. From the hut cross the Glacier de Blanchen NE towards pt.3092 and descend steep crevassed slopes on the right bank of the glacier to gain the more level Otemma glacier. Turn N towards the Petit Mont Collon before making a broad sweep R into the glacier bay enclosed by Petit Mont Collon and the Pointes d'Oren. Continue climbing E towards the Col Petit Mont Collon, 3292m, and ascending the final steep slopes to the col from R to L. Once on the col make a rising traverse S at first and then E to Col de l'Evêque, 3392m, where this route once more merges with the Haute Route.

From the Col de l'Evêque descend gently E towards pt.3263m, keeping R of a crevasse zone and aiming for the Col Collon, 3087m. From L of the Col Collon descend NNE down the Haut Glacier Arolla below the rocky NW face of La Vierge. Descend to c.2900m before traversing E into a glacial bowl below Mont Brulé,

3585m, in the direction of the Col du Mont Brulé, 3213m. In poor visibility the col can be difficult to locate and should not be mistaken for the Col de Tsa de Tsan, which is further S and closer to Mont Brulé. The final 100m to the col are steep, and it is often necessary to kick steps and carry skis. ▶

The Col Mont Brulé marks the border between Switzerland and Italy. From it, make a descending traverse NNE into the upper basin of the Tsa de Tsan glacier, keeping left below the rocks of the Bouquetins Ridge and staying well clear of an impressive icefall on the right. Begin climbing ENE towards the Col de Valpelline 3568m, keeping to the N bank of the Tsa de Tsan Glacier, below the rocks of the South Face of the Tête Blanche 3724m. The glacier steepens gradually, leading finally to the broad slopes of the Col de Valpelline, 3568m, from where it is a short climb along the frontier ridge to the summit of the Tête de Valpelline, 3802m, which is well worth the effort. The view, especially of the Dent d'Herens, is stunning. Return to the col and make a gentle ascent N to the Col de la Tête Blanche, 3600m, from

NB. In the case of retreat, descent can be made to the nearby Bouquetins Hut, which has a stove, fuel and blankets. Alternatively, a descent to Arolla can be made via the Haute Arolla glacier.

Traversing towards the summit of Mont Gelé

Direct Descent to Arolla

If conditions for the Ferpecle glacier are not favourable, it is possible to descend directly to Arolla from the Bertol Hut. The route is via the steep Glacier de Bertol on the W side of the col as far as the Plans de Bertol. From here the ski route turns S, crossing a small shoulder before descending to the Haute Arolla glacier. Note that the lower section does not follow the route of the summer path. At this point the route turns W below the northwest face of Mont Collon (avalanche risk), and descends steeply to the Arolla glacier. Traverse to the centre of the glacier, crossing to the left bank near its snout for a final cruise down the W side of the valley as far as Arolla.

where it is possible to make the short ascent to the summit of the Tête Blanche, 3724m.

Descend NW from the summit to *c.*3600m before turning sharply W towards the Bouquetins ridge. Traverse beneath the Col des Bouquetins before bearing NW to skirt below pt.3229m at the foot of the Dents de Bertol. Maintain height and bear W to the Col de Bertol and the Bertol Hut, 3311m, perched airily above the col to the N. The ladders leading to the hut are accessed from the W side of the col. The views from the hut are magnificent, especially at sunset, when the Dent Blanche in particular is supreme.

Stage 6

Bertol Hut, 3311m – Tête Blanche, 3724m – Wandflue, 3589m – Mota Rota, 3253m– Glacier Ferpecle – Les Haudères, 1452m

Ascent:	550m
Descent:	2250m
Difficulty:	PD+ or AD – depends on the state of the glacier. A serious descent with lots of crevasses and several short, steep pitches – S3.
Principal Aspect:	N, NW
Time:	6–8 hours

If you are unsure about snow conditions for the descent of the Ferpecle glacier it is worth discussing them with the hut guardian, who is also a mountan guide. Good visibility and snow cover are essential for this descent. ◀

To descend the Ferpecle glacier regain the col and retrace your route to below pt.3229m. From here it is possible to make a gently ascending traverse E across the Glacier du Mont Mine to cross a snowy shoulder on the north ridge of the Tête Blanche at pt.3422.6m. From the shoulder a slanting descent can be made towards

the Col d'Herens, 3462m. The same point can be reached by climbing back to the summit of the Tête Blanche, perhaps for sunrise, and skiing down the north ridge of the Tête Blanche to pt.3422.6m before traversing towards the Col d'Herens.

From below the col it is a slight detour to the summit of the Wandfluehorn, 3589m, which offers a magnificent view of the Matterhorn and Dent d'Herens.

From the summit ski NNE over the broad but crevassed slopes of the Plateau d'Herens, skirting R of the Mota Rota rognon, pt.3253. The Glacier de Ferpecle below the rognon is increasingly steep and crevassed. Bear W beneath the rocks of the Mota Rota and its impressive icefall and descend to c.2650m, where the glacier plateaus out. Turn N and continue down the narrowing and still steep glacier, staying R of another serac zone to reach a lower plateau. Descend this more easily to c.2300m and the end of the glacier.

The snout of the glacier is very crevassed, and a way needs to be found to avoid the difficulties. Depending on conditions a way may be found down either the left

The magnificent north face of the Pigne d'Arolla

227

or right bank to avoid the crevasse difficulties. This will lead to a steep gully beneath the snout of the glacier that gives access to easier ground and a small lake below the Glacier du Mont Mine. Continue more easily down the valley past a barrier to Ferpecle and then down the track and road to Les Haudères. Walking this lower section is the likely option later in the season.

AROLLA HIGH-LEVEL CIRCUIT: USEFUL INFORMATION

Huts

Bertol Hut, 3311m.
Tel: 027/83 19 29
Guarded during the spring. Winter room.

Chanrion Hut, 2462m.
Tel: 026/38 12 09
Guarded during the spring. Winter room.

Dix Hut, 2928m.
Tel: 027/81 15 23
Guarded during the spring. Winter room.

Vignettes Hut, 3158m.
Tel: 027/83 13 22
Guarded during the spring. Winter room.

L'Aiguillette Bivouac Hut, 3179m (aka Singla Bivouac)
14 places. No booking possible.

Regondi Bivouac Hut, 2550m
6 places. No phone; no booking possible.

Bouquetins Hut, 2980m
18 places. Unguarded. Wood stove/utensils.

Accommodation in Arolla

Hotel du Mt Collon.
Tel: 027 283 11 91

Michel Rong-Anzevui – Dortoir.
Tel: 027/ 83 15 14

Hotel du Glacier. Hotel and Dortoir. Tel: 027/83 12 18

Useful Contacts

Arolla Office of Tourism.
Tel: 027/83 10 83

Les Haudères Office of Tourism.
Tel: 027/83 10 15

Weather report. Tel: 162

Avalanche bulletin. Tel: 187

Emergency and Rescue

Rega (Swiss).
Tel: 01/383 11 11/14 14

Canton Police. Tel: 117

Italian Police. Tel: 113

ZERMATT AND SAAS FEE 4000ERS

This magnificent high-mountain journey is a genuine *tour de force* that will provide a real challenge to proficient and acclimatised ski mountaineers. The route, as it criss-crosses the mountainous frontier between Switzerland and Italy, offers an opportunity to explore the highest peaks of the Monte Rosa region – all of them 4000ers. Only the Berner Oberland offers similar altitude in quantity and quality. In every sense this memorable tour is the quintessential high-level route.

Success on this venture will demand strong skiing and mountaineering skill in equal measure, along with

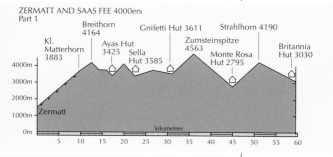

ZERMATT AND SAAS FEE 4000ers
Part 1

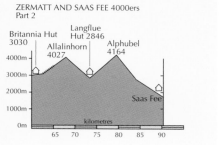

ZERMATT AND SAAS FEE 4000ers
Part 2

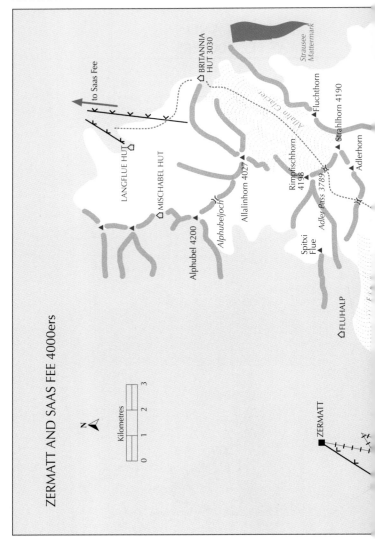

ZERMATT AND SAAS FEE 4000ers

to Saas Fee

BRITANNIA HUT 3030

Strausee
Mattermark

Allalin Glacier

Fluchthorn

Strahlhorn 4190

LANGFLUE HUT

Adlerhorn

MISCHABEL HUT

Allalinhorn 4027

Rimpfischhorn
4198

Alphubeljoch

Adler Pass 3789

Alphubel 4200

Spitxi
Flue

FLUHALP

Kilometres

0   1   2   3

N

ZERMATT

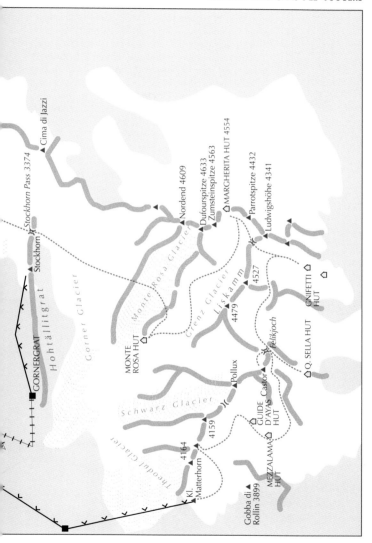

Cima di Jazzi

Stockhorn Pass 3374

Stockhorn

GORNERGRAT

Hohtälligrat

Gorner Glacier

Monte Rosa Glacier

Nordend 4609

Dufourspitze 4633
Zumsteinspitze 4563

MARGHERITA HUT 4554

Parrotspitze 4432

Ludwigshöhe 4341

Grenz Glacier

Liskamm

4527

4479

GNIFETTI HUT

MONTE ROSA HUT

Felikjoch

Q. SELLA HUT

Pollux

Schwarz Glacier

Castor

GUIDE D'AYAS HUT

4159

MEZZALAMA HUT

4164

Theodul Glacier

Kl. Matterhorn

Gobba di Rollin 3899

231

fitness, commitment and considerable luck with weather and conditions – not a lot to ask for really! With much of the route above 3000m it is essential to gain some acclimatisation before setting out. Fortunately Zermatt is an ideal location for a warm-up because it has an extensive lift system and a number of readily accessible summits such as the Cima di Jazzi and Breithorn. That said, Stage 1 of the tour is not particularly strenuous, since it makes maximum use of uplift, and provides an opportunity to climb high while you sleep relatively low.

With a bit of tweaking, and an extra day or two, a fit and ambitious party could bag at least thirteen 4000ers at a reasonable standard, including the Breithorn, Pollux, Castor, Liskamm, Vincent Pyramide, Ludwigshöhe, Parrotspitze, Signalkuppe, Zumsteinspitze, Dufourspitze, Strahlhorn, Allalinhorn and Alphubel. The summits of both Liskamm and Dufourspitze are more difficult than the other peaks mentioned, both being worthy of an AD grade.

Don't underestimate this tour. Throughout it you travel over serious glaciers at high altitude, which

On the summit of the Cima di Jazzi, 3803m, with Castor, Pollux and the long summit ridge of the Breithorn beyond

demands a good level of mountaineering skill and sound judgement. It goes without saying that high winds, icy conditions and poor visibility will bring added dangers and easily make the tour impossible. The route is escapable, but descent – especially on the Italian side – brings logistical problems, as the return from Italy by road is not easy. However, a lower-level traverse using ski lifts can be worked out that will take you back over the Testa Grigia. The good thing about this very high-level tour is that it is possible until very late in the season – right into June, when the days are especially long. I believe the 'via normals' on all Monte Rosa's many tops are much more enjoyable on skis – especially the descents.

The Tour

Start:	Zermatt
Finish:	Saas Fee
Duration:	7 days
Location:	Eastern Pennine Alps. The route begins and ends in Switzerland but crosses into Italy. Many of the peaks climbed straddle the Swiss/Italian frontier.
Difficulty:	BSA. AD. This is a strenuous high-level tour across serious glacier terrain. The ascent of the Doufourspitz and Liskamm involves AD mountaineering; however, both are avoidable.
Best Time:	Mid-March to June
Facilities:	Zermatt has the full range of accommodation and services one would expect of a large internationally renowned ski resort.
Access:	Zermatt, 1600m, is easily reached from the international airports of Geneva, Zurich and even Milan. International rail routes connect to Brig and Visp in the Rhone valley, from where the cog railway climbs steeply to Zermatt in 90 minutes. Motorists can drive as far as Täsch, from where shuttle trains run every 20 minutes to Zermatt. Parking facilities are available in Täsch, as well as in Visp for motorists wishing to continue by rail.

| Maps: | Landeskarte Der Schweiz 1:25,000: Randa 1328, Saas 1329, Matterhorn 1347, Zermatt 1348, Monte Moro 1349. Landeskarte Der Schweiz 1:50,000 Mischabel. IGC 1:50,000 Cervino-Matterhorn e Monte Rosa. |

ROUTE SUMMARY

Stage 1: Kleine Matterhorn, 3883m – Breithorn, 4164m – Guide d'Ayas e Champoluc Hut, 3425m

Stage 2: Guide d'Ayas Hut, 3425m – Castor, 4221m – Quintino Sella Hut, 3585m

Stage 3: Quintino Sella Hut, 3585m – Il Naso, 4150m – Gnifetti Hut, 3611m

Stage 4: Gnifetti Hut, 3611m – Signalkuppe, 4554m – Zumsteinspitze, 4563m – Monte Rosa Hut, 2795m

Stage 5: Monte Rosa Hut, 2795m – Adler pass, 3789m – Strahlhorn, 4190m – Britannia Hut, 3030m

Stage 6: Britannia Hut, 3030m – Allalinhorn, 4027m – Langflue Restaurant/Hut, 2846m

Stage 7: Langflue Restaurant/Hut, 2846m – Alphubel, 4164m – Saas Fee, 1792m, or Täsch, 1450m

ROUTE ITINERARY
Stage 1
Kleine Matterhorn, 3883m – Breithorn, 4164m – Guide d'Ayas e Champoluc Hut, 3425m

Ascent:	279m
Descent:	771m
Difficulty:	SAM. This provides a reasonable warm-up day and takes full advantage of the Kleine Matterhorn lift system. A fit team may wish to include an ascent of Pollux.
Principal Aspect:	S
Time:	4 hours in total (not including Pollux)

If you take the cable car to Kleine Matterhorn, the ascent of the Breithorn is probably the easiest 4000er in the Alps. Despite effortless access, the Breithorn remains a marvellous summit on a fine day. The views are stunning

and the metres skied in descent will always be greater than the ascent – an essential ingredient in a perfect day.

From the top station of the Kleine Matterhorn cable car ski SSE across the Breithorn Plateau, bearing L beneath a ski tow to pt.3795m. Traverse E across the plateau, either skinning or pushing towards the Breithornpass at 3825m. This can be a windswept and wild place, but then the cable car is invariably closed. Nevertheless the surface can be icy and a veritable washboard of sastrugi. When it is, making progress across the plateau is difficult. Before the pass, bear L (NE) to below the south face and summit of the Breithorn. This face can also be windswept and icy, in which case a ski depot is often made close to the bergschrund at the foot of the face, and the final ascent is made on foot.

Whether on skis or foot there is a choice of route to the summit, with snow conditions invariably determining which is best on the day. In good snow conditions the south face offers a straightforward ascent and a delightful descent, and in these conditions a good track will be in place. This is a popular peak for Zermatt's guides.

On the summit of the Breithorn, looking E towards Monte Rosa, Lyskam, Pollux and Castor

The usual ascent route makes a rising traverse from R to L across the south face towards pt.3909m on the shoulder of the mountain. Just before the shoulder turn back R and follow the south-west ridge to the main summit. Make sure you keep well off the crest of the ridge, which is often heavily corniced.

Sometimes conditions favour an alternative route that traverses L to R across the south face to reach the main ridge E of the summit, from where a much narrower ridge is followed to the top. The last section of the ridge is often done on foot.

Descend to the Breithornpass and traverse E towards Pollux aiming to traverse to a point below the tiny Roccia Nera or Rossi e'Volante Bivouac Hut outcrop. At this point turn R and descend S through a zone of crevasses to the Ayas Hut, 3394m. It is possible to make a diagonal descent more directly from the Breithornpass, but this is more exposed to crevasse danger.

If conditions are clear you will have a good view of Castor's west face, and be able to see if it is in condition for an ascent and whether a track is in place.

Traversing the summit ridge of the Zermatt Breithorn. Beyond (L to R) are the peaks of the Dent d'Herens, Matterhorn and Dent Blanche – 4000ers all

Stage 2
Guide d'Ayas Hut, 3425m – Castor, 4221m – Quintino Sella
Hut, 3585m

Ascent:	827m
Descent:	1026m
Difficulty:	SAM. You have a choice of routes depending on conditions. It is possible to reach the Sella Hut without crossing a 4000er. All routes traverse serious glacial terrain.
Principal Aspect:	W and S
Time:	4–6 hours summit; 6–8 hours total

An ascent of the west face of Castor following the line of the normal summer route from the Kleine Matterhorn is possible, but the face is often windswept and icy. It is also steep and exposed.

If conditions are suitable on the west face of Castor ascend in the direction of the Rossi e'Volante Bivouac Hut to c.3700m and then bear R (NE in the direction of the toe of the south-west ridge of Pollux). Aim for the foot of the west face of Castor, making an ascending traverse first from L to R and then back L more or less up the centre of the face, aiming for a point on the ridge N of the main summit. A bergschrund often presents some difficulty, and it is usual to climb the last steep section on foot. Gain the summit, pt.4221m, and then traverse the narrow, undulating and exposed south-east summit ridge over the Felikhorn, 4192m, to the Felikjoch, 4061m.

Alternatively, if the west face is not in condition, a more reliable route is via the Piccolo Verra Glacier, sometimes incorrectly referred to as the Castor Glacier. From the Ayas Hut ski W and then S to reach the Messalama Hut, 3004m. From the hut gain the Piccola Verra glacier and climb E up the E branch of the glacier towards the Punta Perazzi, pt.3906m, between pt.3172m and pt.3191m. Stay close to the centre of the

Traversing towards Pollux and Castor with a stunning backdrop of 4000ers, including (L–R) the Zinal Rothorn, Ober Gablehorn and Weisshorn

glacier, aiming for the Col Perazzi, c.3880m, N of the Punta Perazzi, pt.3906m.

From this col it is possible to climb Castor by ascending NE to the Felikjoch, 4061m, which is reached via its ESE ridge. The final slope to the col is steep. A ski depot is normal at the col. Follow the south-east ridge first over the Felikhorn, 4174m, following the main ridge to the summit of Castor, 4221m – Pollux's heavenly twin! Retrace your steps to the Felikjoch. To reach the Quintino Sella Hut descend from the col and ski initially SW towards the Punta Perazzi and then S down broad glacier slopes to the hut at 3585m.

Stage 3

Quintino Sella Hut, 3585m – Il Naso, 4150m – Gnifetti Hut, 3611m

From the hut ascend NE on the narrow Felik glacier passing between pt.3846m and pt.3744m to gain the west bay of the Lis Glacier. Continue climbing NE, crossing a wide glacier plateau underneath Liskamm's south face.

Ascent:	515m
Descent:	453m
Difficulty:	BSA. PD. A high-altitude traverse crossing complex and often steep terrain. An enjoyable combination is the traverse of Il Naso with an ascent of the Vincent Pyramid.
Principal Aspect:	S, W and SE
Time:	2–3 hours to Il Naso. 4–5 hours in total.

Carry on going E as far as the foot of the snow dome of Il Naso. Climb steeply up the west flank to gain the Passo del Nasso, a vague glacial col, *c.*4150m, on the south flank of the glacial boss of Il Naso itself. This can feel exposed and delicate in icy conditions.

Continue E and then NE on a traverse of Il Naso until below the vague SE ridge of a snow dome, where it is possible to descend steeply onto the east branch of the Lis glacier. This is well crevassed, and the bergschrund may be awkward if open. Continue traversing in an arc SE towards the Vincent Pyramid before turning S to descend to the Gnifetti Hut.

Castor's massive north-west face seen from Pollux – a track up this standard but steep normal route leads to the ridge left of the main summit

Perfect powder conditions below the north face of Pollux during a descent of the Schwartz glacier

Stage 4

Gnifetti Hut, 3611m – Signalkuppe, 4554m – Zumsteinspitze, 4563m – Monte Rosa Hut, 2795m

Ascent:	916m
Descent:	1768m
Difficulty:	SAM. PD. A strenuous ski-mountaineering day at high altitude. The descent is through complex and serious glacial terrain, which is best attempted in good visibility even when a track is already in place.
Principal Aspect:	S and W
Time:	5–6 to the Zumsteinspitze. 8–10 total

From the hut climb N on the Garstelet glacier, skirting the west flank of the Vincent Pyramid to reach the upper basin of the east branch of the Lis glacier. Continue N towards the Lisjoch, 4151m, but at c.4100m bear R (NE) to a second broad unnamed col, pt.4246m, below the north-west ridge of the Ludwigshöhe. This is in a splendid position surrounded by 4000m summits.

Descend slightly to the NE into the huge upper basin of the Grenz glacier. At c.4200m climb NE in a glacier bowl diagonally rightwards to the Col Gnifetti, pt.4452m, which is between the Signalkuppe and Zumsteinspitze. Both peaks are easily reached from this col.

For the Zumsteinspitze climb as high as possible on skis and then crampon up the south-east ridge, which is

Finding a route through a crevasse on the Grentz glacier

The Signalkuppe, 4554m, Parrotspitze, 4432m, and Luwigs-höhe, 4341m, seen from the summit ridge of the Lyskamm, 4479m

the frontier between Switzerland and Italy, to reach the summit. Return to the col and either skin or crampon SE across a steep snow face to reach the summit of the Signalkuppe and the Margherita Hut. Return to the Gnifetti Col.

From the col retrace your track towards the unnamed col, pt.4246m, to *c.*4200m. Instead of climbing to the col, turn R (W) and in a wide arc ski NW towards pt.3753m at the toe of Monte Rosa's south-west ridge, which leads to the Sattel of the Dufourspitze. Between *c.*4000m and 3800m there is a heavily crevassed area that demands much care. Descend the right bank (N) of the glacier between an icefall and the south-west ridge of the Dufourspitze. Below 3800m the slope eases into a broad snow plateau. Continue skiing NW towards pt.3699m before sweeping L (W) towards the impressive north face of Liskamm to evade an area of seracs and crevasses. Keep these to the R (N). At *c.*3400m, where the terrain moderates, you should bear NW towards pt.3109m and the rocks of the Ob Plattje. Continue descending NW following a well-defined lateral moraine or the mulde on its R to the Monte Rosa Hut.

Stage 5
Monte Rosa Hut, 2795m – Adler Pass, 3789m – Strahlhorn, 4190m – Britannia Hut, 3030m

Ascent:	1395m
Descent:	1161m
Difficulty:	SAM. PD. Yet another long day spent snaking through complex glacial terrain. The final slope to the Adler pass is steep, exposed and often icy.
Principal Aspect:	W and E
Time:	5½–6 hours to the Adler pass. 8–10 hours total

From the Monte Rosa Hut traverse NE and then SE to gain a hollow E of a well-marked lateral moraine on the true right bank of the Monte Rosa glacier. At c.2900m turn L (NE) and cross the lower part of the glacier and begin climbing moraines at c.3000m. Continue climbing N to gain the crest of a rock rib that falls from pt.3263. The next section is usually done on foot. Climb the crest for c.50m as far as 3060m and descend the far side to reach the true left bank of the Gorner glacier.

Ascend NW in the direction of the Stockhorn pass, 3394m, which connects the Gorner and Findel glaciers. At the pass turn L (N) and descend to pt.3120m in the centre of the Findel glacier. Continue traversing NNE, crossing the glacier to reach the foot of a steep snow slope dividing the rocky south ridge of the Adlerhorn, 3988m, between pt.3421m and the Strahlchnubel, pt.3222m. Ascend this steep slope to gain the Adler glacier. Traverse N to the true right bank of the Adler glacier at 3400m, keeping below the south face of the Rimpfischhorn. Continue the steep ascent towards the Adler pass, aiming to climb it from L to R. This final slope is abrupt and exposed to the wind, and is often icy. Although it can be climbed on skis, most sensible parties opt for the safety of crampons and the security of a rope.

From the Adler pass the Strahlhorn is an easy ascent and adds 1–2 hours to the total. The descent returns more or less to the pass before descending NE down the true left bank of the Allalin glacier under the rockwall of the Rimpfischhorn and the Hohlaubgrat of the Allalinhorn. At pt.3143.3 turn N to cross the Hohlaub glacier in a gently descending traverse to a point below the Hinter

Looking towards the Adler pass between the peaks of the Rimpfisschhorn, 4198m, and the Strahlhorn, 4190m, from across the Findel glacier

Allalin ridge, from where a final short, sharp climb leads to the Britannia Hut, 3029m.

From the Britannia Hut a track leads NW to the Felskin ski lift and pistes that can be followed to Saas Fee (1–2 hrs).

Stage 6
Britannia Hut, 3030m – Allalinhorn, 4027m – Langflue Restaurant/Hut, 2846m

Ascent:	From hut, 997m; From Metro top station, 571m
Descent:	1157m, plus 39m to Metro middle station
Difficulty:	SAM. F+. Said to be the 4000er most visited by skiers – a good summit nevertheless, with an outstanding descent to the valley.
Principal Aspect:	N and W
Time:	3–4 hours to summit

From the hut follow a well-pisted track to the top of the Felskinn ski lift and the tunnel leading to lower station of the Mittel Allalin underground railway lift.

From the top station of the Mittelallalin ascend SW

towards the Feechopf. To begin there is normally a pisted track, but this is soon left as you climb towards the Feejoch. Depending on the state of the bergschrund, pass it on either the left or right to reach the col. The summit snow cone varies from season to season. The usual route makes a rising traverses across the south flank to below the summit before a final steeper climb leads to a hollow below the peak on the south side. Make a ski depot here, and crampon along the ridge to the summit cross. When the final cone is icy, it is best to make a ski depot early and crampon up the south or south-west ridge to the summit.

Descend on skis to the Feejoch. Then, either descend via the route of ascent to the Mittelallalin and then follow pistes to the Langfluehut, 2870m; or, from the Feejoch, traverse NE well above the bergschrund keeping above a line of seracs on the west flank of the Allalinhorn until close to pt.3597m. At a point where it is possible to turn L (W) descend a fine slope to the R of the seracs. Continue descending but bearing N down the Fee glacier, through a zone of crevasses, keeping L of the pisted slopes if conditions are good until forced to join the piste and descend to the Langflue Hut. Alternatively join the piste early, always bearing L and descend to the hut.

On the summit of the Allalinhorn

Stage 7
Langflue Restaurant/Hut, 2846m – Alphubel, 4164m – Saas
Fee, 1792m, or Täsch, 1450m

Ascent:	1336m
Descent:	2406m to Saas Fee; 2756m to Täsch
Difficulty:	SAM. PD-. Possible to finish in Saas Fee or, given good snow conditions, descend to Täsch and all but close the circle back to Zermatt on skis.
Principal Aspect:	E, NE, also W if descending to Täsch
Time:	4–5 hours to the summit

From the hut ascend SW, passing under the ski lift, and ascend a branch of the Fee glacier contained between two rocky ribs extending from the Feechofp and the Alphubel towards the Langflue Hut. Gain the glacier and climb the first step, normally from R to L. Above this first step bear generally R, passing through a crevasse zone at c.3400m. Pass by a serac barrier by following an ice ramp bearing from R to L, which leads eventually to an upper snow basin that then continues more easily to the Alphubeljoch. Instead of ascending S towards the joch turn R (NE) above the crevasse zone and climb the long but regular snow slope of the east flank of the Alphubel.

Conditions will determine the route on the upper section, which in certain years is highly crevassed and requires a number of long detours to find the best route. The final step is really a broad glacial couloir leading to the summit snows. It good snow conditions it is possible to skin to the summit, but in hard snow or icy conditions the final climb is best done in crampons.

Descent to Saas Fee: From the summit descend by the same route to the Langflue, from where there are several obvious pisted and off-piste options descending to Saas Fee.

Descent to Täsch: Either continue towards the Alphubeljoch instead of climbing the Alphubel or, from the summit of the Alphubel, descend the steep upper slopes and then make a descending traverse SSE to reach the Alphubeljoch.

From the pass descend W onto the upper Alphubel glacier. Continue W towards pt.3510m, bearing L (S) at *c.*3600 to descend steeper slopes leading to the southern branch of the Alphubel glacier. The northern branch of the Alphubel glacier below the S wall of the Rotgrat is highly crevassed and not recommended, even though it seems more direct. At *c.*3500m, turn R (NW) towards pt.3094m. At the end of the glacier descend a series of steep steps to gain the Terrace de Chummiboden (2886m), leading to the hut. From the hut make a descending traverse NW across the steep flank of the Rinderberg descending to Ottavan, 2214m. In a good season it may be possible to descend on skis all the way to Täsch via Eggenstadel and Resti.

ZERMATT AND SAAS FEE 4000ERS: USEFUL INFORMATION

Huts

Guide d'Ayas e Champoluc Hut, 3394m. Tel: 0125/308083. Tel: 0125/308975/308960

Quintino Sella Hut, 3585m, CAI. Tel: 0125 36 61 13

Gniffetti Hut, 3647m. Tel: 0163/78015. Tel: 016354384

Monte Rosa Hut, 2795m, CAS. Tel: 028 67 21 15

Britannia Hut, 3030m, CAS. Tel: 028 57 22 88

Langflue Hut (owned by the Saas commune). Tel: 02857 21 32

Hoh Saas Hut. Tel: 027/ 957 17 13

Useful Contacts

Zermatt Tourist Office. Tel: 027/966 81 00 www.zermatt.ch

Saas Fee Tourist Office. Tel: 027/958 1858 www.saas-fee.ch

Park Hotel, Saas Fee. Tel: 027 957 24 26

Garni Hotel, Imseng. Tel: 027 958 12 58

Emergency and Rescue

Rega (Swiss). Tel: 01/383 11 11/14 14

Police (Swiss). Tel: 117

Police (Italian). Tel: 113

SUMMARY OF THE TOURS

Tour	Country	Grade	Duration
Ecrins Haute Route	France	BSA. AD	7 days
Haute Maurienne Traverse	France	SAM/BSA. PD+ with AD option	5 days
La Poulé – Vanoise High-Level Circuit	France	SAM/BSA. PD+ with D option	5–6 days
Grand Paradiso Haute Route	Italy	SAM. PD+	7 days
Mont Blanc Haute Route	Switzerland, Italy, France	BSA. AD+ with D option	7 days
Mont Blanc Day Tours	France, Switzerland	SAM/BSA. PD to D	
Classic Haute Route	France, Switzerland	SAM/BSA. PD+ to AD-	7–8 days
Verbier High-Level Route	Switzerland	SAM. PD	4–5 days
Arolla High-Level Circuit	Switzerland, Italy	SAM/BSA	6 days
Zermatt and Saas Fee 4000ers	Switzerland, Italy	BSA	6 days

Total Ascent	Total Descent	Best Period	Type
5936m	8601m	March–May	Circular
4598m	4538m	Feb–May	Circular
6880m	8510m	Feb-May	Circular
7725m	7808m	March–May	Linear
8980m	4340m	April–June	Linear
		Jan–May	Day tours
10,869m including Grande Lui	13,332m	March–May	Linear
4013m	7568m	March–May	Linear
6620m	7532m	March–May	Circular
6265m	8742m	March–June	Linear or circular

FURTHER READING AND INFORMATION

Avalanche Awareness

Snow Sense by Jill Fredston and Doug Fesler (Alaska Mountain Safety Centre) ISBN 0964399407 – this is one of the best, no-nonsense books on the subject I've read.

The ABC of Snow Safety by E.R. La Chapelle (Mountaineers books) – another must-read book on avalanche awareness.

The Avalanche Handbook by McLung and Schaerer (Cordee) ISBN 0898863643

Avalanche Safety For Skiers and Climbers by T. Daffern (Diadem/Rocky Mountain Books) ISBN 0906371260

Skiing

Ski Powder by Martin Epp (Fernhurst)

Skiing and the Art of Carving by Ellen Post Foster (Turning Point ski foundation) ISBN 0964739038

Ski Mountaineering Guided Tours and Training

O'Connor Adventure, www.oconnoradventure.com

Avalanche Awareness Training

O'Connor Adventure, www.oconnoradventure.com

European Avalanche School, www.avaschool.com

Snow and Avalanche Research Davos, www.slf.ch/slf/slf.html

Canadian Avalanche Association, www.csac.org

Scottish Avalanche Information Service, www.sais.gov.uk

ALPINE SKI MOUNTAINEERING, VOLUME 2: CENTRAL AND EASTERN ALPS

Deep, deep snow in Realp at the start of the Tour Soleil

Features:

Western Bernese Alps Traverse

Oberland North

Bernese Oberland 4000ers

Tour Soleil

Urner Haute Route

Albula Alps Traverse

Bernina High-Level Route

Silvretta Traverse

Ortler Grand Circuit

Ötztal High-Level Route

Stubai High Level Route

LISTING OF CICERONE GUIDES

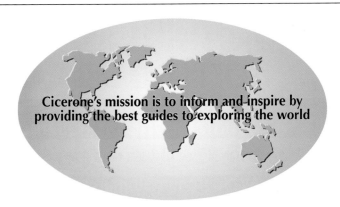

Cicerone's mission is to inform and inspire by providing the best guides to exploring the world

Since its foundation over 30 years ago, Cicerone has specialised in publishing guidebooks and has built a reputation for quality and reliability. It now publishes nearly 300 guides to the major destinations for outdoor enthusiasts, including Europe, UK and the rest of the world.

Written by leading and committed specialists, Cicerone guides are recognised as the most authoritative. They are full of information, maps and illustrations so that the user can plan and complete a successful and safe trip or expedition – be it a long face climb, a walk over Lakeland fells, an alpine traverse, a Himalayan trek or a ramble in the countryside.

With a thorough introduction to assist planning, clear diagrams, maps and colour photographs to illustrate the terrain and route, and accurate and detailed text, Cicerone guides are designed for ease of use and access to the information.

If the facts on the ground change, or there is any aspect of a guide that you think we can improve, we are always delighted to hear from you.

Cicerone Press
2 Police Square Milnthorpe Cumbria LA7 7PY
Tel:01539 562 069   Fax:01539 563 417
e-mail:info@cicerone.co.uk   web:www.cicerone.co.uk

CICERONE